Exchange TRADED PROFITS

CASHING IN on new ETF Trading Methods

DAVID VOMUND

Marketplace Books
Glenelg, Maryland

Publisher: Chris Myers
VP/General Manager: John Boyer
Senior Editor: Courtney Jenkins
Editorial Coordinator: Danielle Hainsey
Art Director: Larry Strauss
Graphic Designer: Jennifer Marin
Production Design Interns: Jessica Weedlun & Morgan Di Pietro

Copyright © 2011 by David Vomund

Published by Marketplace Books Inc.

All rights reserved.

Reproduction or translation of any part of this work beyond that permitted by section 107 or 108 of the 1976 United States Copyright Act without the permission of the copyright owner is unlawful. Requests for permission or further information should be addressed to the Permissions Department at Marketplace Books®.

This publication is designed to provide accurate and authoritative information in regard to the subject matter covered. It is sold with the understanding that neither the author nor the publisher is engaged in rendering legal, accounting, or other professional service. If legal advice or other expert assistance is required, the services of a competent professional person should be sought.

From a Declaration of Principles jointly adopted by a Committee of the American Bar Association and a Committee of Publishers.

ISBN: 1-59280-4500
ISBN 13: 978-1-592-80-4504

Printed in the United States of America.

Table of Contents

Preface   v

Chapter 1: ETF Basics   1

Chapter 2: Mechanical Trading Models   13

Chapter 3: Adding Insightful Chart Pattern Analysis   51

Chapter 4: Point & Figure Charting   61

Chapter 5: Technical Indicators and ETF Volume   73

Chapter 6: Market Timing   95

Chapter 7: Portfolio Management   117

Chapter 8: Trading Psychology and the Personal Trading Plan   137

Appendix: Two ETF Options Strategies   145

Recommended Reading   161

Glossary   167

About David Vomund   173

Preface

*"Those who cannot remember the past
are condemned to repeat it."*

—George Santayana

This has been one memorable decade. The Dow crossed the 10,000 level in both 1999 and 2009. Two of the largest bear markets occurred during this period. Many traditional investment theories, including those taught in prestigious university MBA programs, have not worked. For many, investment portfolios have been devastated. Lifestyles have changed.

Despite these changes, we find people are still following the same investment approaches. It is as if they have not learned any lessons from the market's behavior.

The best time to evaluate your investment approach is after a bear market. Bear markets reveal chinks in the armor. Shortly after the 2000 to 2002 bear market, I evaluated the lessons learned and began using exchange-traded funds (ETFs) as the exclusive investment vehicle for my Style Index Portfolios managed account program. Making that change has served me well.

Style Index Portfolios hold securities that track various market indexes. These "style indexes" include large-cap growth, large-cap value, small-cap growth, small-cap value, and international. Trading style indexes allows me to rotate to the market segments showing the best performance. When growth is in favor, my portfolios rotate toward growth-oriented indexes. When value is in favor, my portfolios rotate to value-oriented indexes. Unlike most other managers, I am not locked into one investment style.

After the 2007 to 2009 bear market, I once again took the time to evaluate the lessons learned. Here are three of the biggest:

1. Diversification is overrated.

Building a diversified portfolio has long been the selling point of professional money managers. A diversified portfolio is one in which many securities are held, and the securities move independently of one another. The theory is that some parts of a portfolio will always increase, offsetting some or all of the losses in the other areas.

The problem is that during bad markets, securities that moved independently of one another all of a sudden become more correlated. In 2008, those who took comfort in being diversified were disheartened to see losses in nearly all areas of their portfolio. U.S. Treasury Bonds rose while every other major asset class fell. The projected benefits of adding small-cap stocks, international stocks, real estate investment trusts, corporate bonds, commodities, and precious metals vanished during the market decline. They didn't zig when the market zagged.

Seeing spikes in correlation is nothing new. Securities that once moved independently of one another tend to move in lockstep during times of extreme market stress. That means that portfolios are diversified in bull markets (i.e., periods when diversification is not needed), but then act as if they are not diversified in bear markets (i.e., periods when diversification *is* needed).

The next time a professional advisor shows you a glossy pie chart on the benefits of diversification, notice that the correlation studies will cover times when diversification is not needed. If it did not work in the last bear market, why should we expect it to work in the next bear market?

2. Buying and holding a large-cap index is not necessarily the best approach.

A view shared by most academics and large institutions is that one is best served by simply buying and holding the S&P 500. That is why the Vanguard Index 500 is the largest mutual fund, and the S&P 500 SPDR is the largest ETF.

It is easy to see why this approach grew in popularity in the 1980s and 1990s. For the 18-year period between 1982 and 2000, the S&P 500 returned more than 2,117 percent, according to Ibbotson Associates, a leading authority on asset allocation. Then came the 2000s.

Parents who began saving for their children's college education have nothing to show for it. College savings plans, which allow for tax-free growth, actually have losses. Yes, stocks increase over the long run, but the definition of long run has changed.

It gets worse. Adjusted for inflation, the Dow Jones Industrial Average was unchanged from 1966 to March 8, 2009. It is not that the market was bad during this period. After all, the Dow was around 1,000 in 1966! Adjusted for inflation, however, buying and holding has not created the wealth that one would expect.

A more active approach is needed. In this book, we demonstrate that returns can be greatly improved by periodically rotating to different market indexes.

3. In any market environment, there will always be a sector that does well.

This is the lesson I learned from the recent bear market. I previously held the belief that a sector-rotation portfolio could do well in any market environment. In bad markets, there would often be a sector—maybe energy or metals—that would do well. But it is not always so. In 2008, all the Fidelity sector funds and the entire sector ETF list that I track lost value.

By trading sector funds, your portfolio can be less dependent on the market's movement; but a truly all-weather portfolio, one that can go up in any market environment, requires the use of inverse ETFs.

The new breed of ETFs, such as sector, commodity, currency, and inverse ETFs, allows investors to be more flexible with their portfolios. Learning lessons from past bear markets, we can use these ETFs to create strategies that investors were unable to apply just five years ago. By making a trade or two a month, portfolio results can far exceed those that buy and hold a market index. By overweighting a portfolio in a few select ETFs, investors can build wealth that is not offset by inflation. By holding a few select ETFs, investors can succeed in all market environments. That is what this book is about. Enjoy.

Exchange TRADED PROFITS

1 ETF Basics

Exchange-traded funds (ETFs) have exploded in popularity. When I wrote *ETF Trading Strategies Revealed* in 2006, few people outside Wall Street knew what ETFs were. That has changed. ETFs now represent about 20 percent of all trading volume in the U.S. equities market. Often, half of the most active securities on a given day are ETFs. Back in 2006, commodity, inverse, and leveraged ETFs were just being introduced. Now they are important components of many institutional portfolios.

In this book, we assume that readers understand the basics of how ETFs work and how one invests in them. Our focus here is on how to make money by trading ETFs. That said, this chapter will provide a brief background on ETFs.

> **More Info**
>
> For more information on the basics of ETFs, please consult the Recommended Reading section at the end of this book.

HISTORY

ETFs were introduced in the United States in 1993 with the advent of the Standard & Poor's Depositary Receipt, commonly known as the S&P 500 Spyder (SPY). Now there are over 900 ETFs in the marketplace. This does not mean you need to be aware of or track all 900-plus funds. Many of these ETFs are not well-owned, have very little trading volume, and may be closed due to little interest.

DEFINITION

ETFs are securities that combine elements of index funds, but do so with a twist. Like index funds, ETFs are pools of securities that track specific market indexes at a very low cost. Like stocks, ETFs are traded on major U.S. stock exchanges and can be bought and sold anytime during normal trading hours.

Similar to index funds, most ETFs represent ownership in an underlying portfolio of securities that tracks a specific market index. That index may cover an entire market or sections of the market broken down by capitalization, sector, style, country, etc.

COST

When it comes to running an investment fund, there will always be costs. These costs can include analyst fees, marketing costs, and administrative costs. Generally, index funds are cheaper to run than actively managed funds. Because most ETFs are index funds, their expenses are typically well below those of actively managed mutual funds. Even when you compare similar products, ETF expenses are generally lower. For example, the Vanguard Index 500 mutual fund has a very low expense ratio of 0.18 percent of assets, but the SPDR S&P 500 ETF is cheaper still, with an expense ratio of 0.10 percent.

ETFs are typically more tax-efficient than mutual funds. Mutual funds sometimes have to sell holdings to meet the need of redemptions. That triggers a capital gains distribution for all fund shareholders. Anyone who bought a mutual fund in early December and ended up paying taxes on other people's gains knows that's no fun!

With ETFs, shares are bought and sold on the open market, so if one investor cashes out, it does not affect others. The vast majority of equity ETFs do not pay capital gains distributions, but there are exceptions. The most notable are inverse and leveraged funds. ETFs that trade futures and swaps contracts are prone to capital gains distributions.

Still, there may be overriding reasons for favoring mutual funds for some investors. For example, if you invest small sums at regular intervals, then mutual funds are more appropriate. Because ETFs trade like stocks, investors pay a brokerage commission each time they buy or sell, making these funds expensive for people who add regularly to their investments.

> *ETFs can provide a cost-effective method of investment, but it is important to consider tax efficiency, brokerage fees, and all of the costs involved before making a trade.*

GROWTH

The early stage of ETF growth is over. The iShares and State Street families captured market share by being the first to introduce ETFs in popular categories. Latecomers have little chance because investors rightfully flock to the ETF with high volume. For example, iShares Small Cap Russell 2000 ETF (IWM) was introduced in May 2000 and averages over 70 million shares per day. The PowerShares Small Cap ETF (PZJ) was introduced in February 2006 and only averages 20,000 shares per day. Which would you rather buy?

To further growth, ETF families are introducing special niche ETFs, which may or may not resonate with investors. Claymore has done well with its solar energy ETF (TAN), and ProShares has built its thriving business on leveraged and inverse ETFs. But many other niche ETFs are being introduced to little or no fanfare. They won't last long.

VOLUME

Trading volume matters. That is because there is a link between trading volume and spreads.

> The "**spread**" refers to the difference between the bid and ask prices.

Most people focus on the brokerage commission as the cost of trading ETFs. The larger cost, however, can be the spread. One can think of this cost as how much you would lose if you bought and then immediately sold a security, excluding the commission cost. Because buy orders are executed near the asking price and sell orders are executed near the bid price, there will be a loss in the trade. The larger the difference between the bid and ask price, the larger the loss.

The good news is the vast majority of ETFs have low spreads. The largest ETFs typically have spreads of 0.05 percent or less. Only the small and thinly traded ETFs have large spreads. I like to see ETFs trade at least 100,000 a day. The more they trade, the better it is. I have little interest in light-volume ETFs.

LIQUIDITY

A liquid investment is one that can quickly be bought and sold at its fair market value. Individual purchases and sales of the security should not affect its price.

The higher the volume, the more liquid the security.

The importance of ETF volume and liquidity came into play during the "flash crash"—when the market briefly plunged 1,000 points on May 6, 2010. An unsettling number of ETFs fell faster than the indexes they were tracking. Most of these were low-volume ETFs, and market makers would often help the liquidity in these securities. When market makers stop working, as they temporarily did during the flash crash, then prices can swing wildly.

Fortunately, ETFs are generally more liquid than stocks. If an ETF and a stock both have the same price and trade 35,000 shares on a particular day, the ETF will typically be more liquid. That is, your order is much less likely to move the price.

ETFs are more liquid than stocks because, unlike stocks, the number of shares in an ETF is not fixed. If the demand for a given ETF outstrips supply at any point, then a specialist may simply create new shares from a basket of the underlying securities in that fund. Shares are created or redeemed to meet demand. Therefore, the liquidity of an ETF is defined not only by its volume, but also by the liquidity of its holdings.

> *The liquidity of an ETF is defined not only by its volume, but also by the liquidity of its holdings.*

For client portfolios, I have periodically purchased or sold ETFs where more than half of the total volume was a result of my block order. Expecting that it would take a long time to get a fair execution, I have been pleasantly surprised to get immediate execution at the market price. Figure 1.1, which shows a one-minute bar chart of iShares Small-Cap Value (IJS), is a good example. When I placed my buy order, I expected that it would take several minutes to complete the execution. Although my block trade swamped previous volume (see arrow on the volume chart), my limit order was filled at the prevailing price.

Figure 1.1

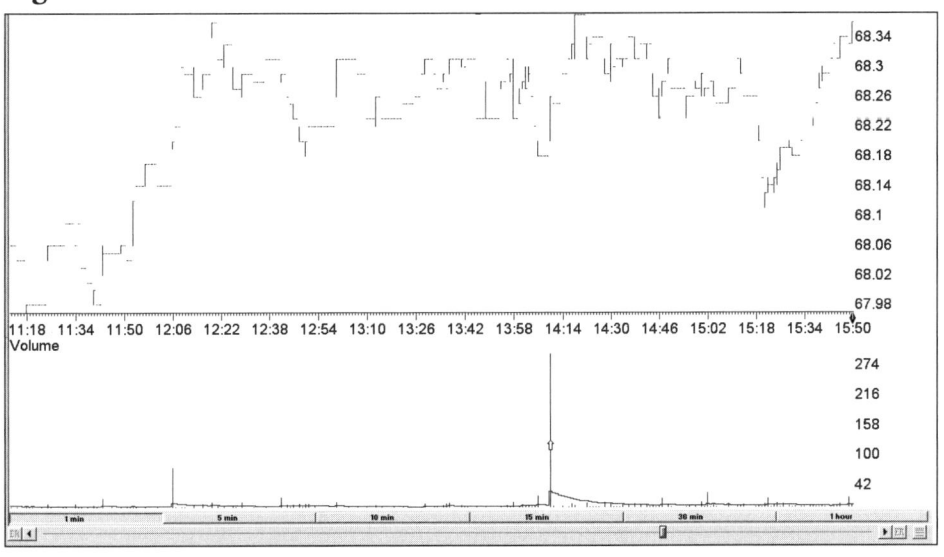

One-Minute Bar Chart of iShares Small-Cap Value (IJS), showing immediate execution at the market price. | Courtesy AIQ

When you place a trade in a low-volume ETF, do not use a market order. Instead, place a limit order between the bid and the ask price. Unless it is a fast-moving market, you will almost always get a quick execution.

EXCHANGE-TRADED NOTES

Exchange-traded notes (ETNs) look and feel like ETFs, but have their own advantages. They allow the common individual investor to buy difficult-to-reach market segments, such as commodities. Before the 2008 financial crisis, the future of ETNs looked bright. Darkness has since set in.

Whereas ETFs are backed by their portfolio holdings (i.e., investors would be made whole by their claims on the stocks held by the ETF), ETNs are backed by the credit of the issuing bank, and so they are only as good as the debt of their backing bank. In February 2008, Lehman Brothers introduced several ETNs under the Opta brand name. When Lehman closed its doors, so did its ETNs. Shareholders joined the long line of Lehman creditors.

The next stone to hit the ETN market came in 2009 when the Commodity Futures Trading Commission began placing restrictions on some commodity ETF and ETNs. Although the outlook for commodity-based products is unclear as of this writing, it does seem certain that commodity funds will either face harsh restrictions or may even be forced to close their doors altogether. That's a shame.

Part of the problem is that the prices of many commodity funds are deviating from the index that they are supposed to track. What investors are learning is that it is not possible to match the performance of a diversified commodity index. That is because these indexes track futures contracts—but futures contracts expire, and rolling-over to the next contract is costly.

With the exception of gold, silver, and other precious metals, a commodity ETF cannot physically hold the commodity in its portfolio. Instead, they invest in the commodity's futures contract. These contracts expire so the ETF continually rolls the funds to the next contract. This rolling-over is hurting the performance of most commodity funds and it is causing their prices to badly deviate from their tracking index. For this reason, ETFs that trade futures contracts are generally not good buy-and-hold choices. Instead, consider funds that physically hold the commodity, like SPDR Gold Trust (GLD) and iShares Comex Gold (IAU).

When it comes to buying a commodity ETF or ETN, be sure that you understand what it tracks. An oil fund, for example, can track energy stocks, nearest-month oil futures contracts, or futures contracts with different expiration periods. Performance will vary depending on its structure.

LEVERAGED AND INVERSE ETFS

The fastest-growing ETF segment is leveraged and inverse ETFs. It is easy to see why. These ETFs allow investors to use leverage without borrowing, or move inverse the market without shorting. The ProShares family of ETFs dominates this marketplace.

Leveraged and inverse funds are designed to achieve a multiple of index returns on a daily basis. A double-leveraged long fund will move twice as fast as the index it tracks. A double-leveraged short fund will move twice as fast as and in the opposite direction from the index it tracks.

Although lawyers may say these funds are working as advertised, most investors would disagree. Suppose someone had the foresight to predict that the 2008 bear market would be caused by falling real estate values. He surely would want to buy ProShares UltraShort Real Estate (SRS). If he bought SRS on October 1, 2008, right before the financial collapse, and held it through the rest of that year, he would have lost 30 percent.

Suppose he also predicted that China would be one of the worst-hit countries. The long China ETF lost nearly half its value from mid-March 2008 through October 2008. In that environment, surely the ProShares UltraShort China (FXP) was a good play. Not so fast. Over the same period, FXP lost nearly 20 percent of its value.

What is going on? The ETFs are designed to match the daily return of their benchmark indexes. The manager of the fund typically holds stocks, index futures, swaps, or short positions along with cash equivalents to achieve this daily fund objective on an ongoing basis. So on a given day, if the index is down 1.5 percent, then the double-leveraged inverse ETF should be up about 3 percent.

Over longer periods, however, the returns will not match due to compounding. Adding and subtracting the daily percentage returns over a month will not equal the percentage change for that month. Tracking results worsen in periods of high volatility, and the fourth quarter of 2008 was an exceptionally volatile quarter. As a result of poor performance in late 2008, many are saying that these vehicles should not be a part of a portfolio—for example, UBS no longer allows its advisors to place client money in them. I am not in that camp.

> *Leveraged and inverse ETFs are designed to track the daily return of their benchmark indexes. Over longer periods, however, the returns will not match due to compounding.*

There is an assumption that compounding will always hurt a fund's performance. Not so fast. Suppose a double-leveraged fund rises ten percent three days in a row. Its return would be 33.1 percent. Assuming the index rose five percent on each of those days, the leveraged three-day return was more than double the 15.8 percent return on the index. Strong uptrending markets are a leveraged fund's friend.

What about downtrending markets? Let's reverse the earlier example. If an inverse double-leveraged fund fell ten percent three days in a row, it would have a 27.1 percent loss. That's less negative than double the 14.26 percent loss of the unleveraged investment. Leveraged ETFs can even outperform on the downside.

The problem comes in volatile markets. As a simple example, let's say the ETF rises by ten percent one day and then falls ten percent the next. The investor has a one percent loss, even though summing the individual returns lead to a value of zero. In volatile markets, leveraged ETFs can lose more than what the index suggests. In extreme cases, these ETFs can lose money even when the index rises. That is what happened in 2008.

> *Strong uptrending markets are a leveraged fund's friend, and leveraged ETFs can even outperform on the downside. The problem comes in volatile markets.*

Because of bad press and client dissatisfaction, changes are being made to these instruments. New ETFs that rebalance positions on a monthly, instead of daily, basis are being introduced. This should reduce the longer-term tracking error, but there are risks here, too. As prices fluctuate, the degree of leverage will change. In volatile markets, a fund could have a significantly higher degree of leverage than what is advertised.

Overall, many say that leveraged and inverse ETFs should not be held for more than one day. I would not go that far. If the market is collapsing, I am willing to hold an inverse ETF for more than one day. One should ignore the performance of the underlying index and perform a buy-and-sell analysis on the ETF itself. If you buy low and sell high, then you should not care if it did not track an index. That said, leveraged ETFs and inverse ETFs are not good buy-and-hold instruments, and if they are held for more than a month, it will often pay to rebalance them.

> *Ignore the performance of the underlying index and perform a buy-and-sell analysis on the ETF itself.*

Finally, it should be noted that there is a hidden credit risk on leveraged ETFs. A double-leveraged ETF cannot hold a basket of equities that is twice the size of its index. Instead, swaps derivatives are used to capture the desired daily leveraged returns. These swaps are contracts traded through investment banks. That is fine unless a bank collapses. There is counterparty risk if an institution fails to honor a contract. An ETF would not lose its entire principal, but if a bank that guarantees the swaps contract collapses, then the ETF will lose part of its value.

FINAL THOUGHTS

There are good reasons why ETFs have exploded in popularity. ETFs allow investors to quickly buy and sell market indexes, specific sectors, individual countries, commodities, and even currencies. Institutional investors realize their potential and ETFs are playing an ever more important role in their portfolios. Individual investors can follow strategies that were not previously possible without going to the futures market. Chapter 2 will offer some of these strategies.

Quick Quiz

1) The management fees for S&P 500 index ETFs are generally _____ those on S&P 500 index mutual funds.

   a. greater than

   b. less than

   c. equal to

2) What additional risk do ETNs have compared to ETFs?

   a. Their holdings are always riskier.

   b. They are backed by the credit of the issuer.

   c. One can only buy and sell at the close.

   d. They generally have less volume than ETFs.

3) Why does a leveraged ETF move away from its tracking index over longer periods of time?

   a. Because futures products are used.

   b. Because the supply of shares often changes.

   c. Because of compounding.

For the answers to this quiz, please visit the Trader's Library Education Corner online at www.TradersLibrary.com/TLEcorner.

2   Mechanical Trading Models

In the 1970s, NFL quarterbacks called their own plays. At the time, I was a fan of the Oakland Raiders. Their coach knew the first play of every game would be a run off left tackle. After that, it was up to Ken Stabler, the quarterback, to call the plays. And why not have the quarterback call the plays? He is the one who is in the trenches and has the feel of the game.

Today, quarterbacks are told what plays to call. Most stick to the signals given to them from the sidelines. A few veterans, however, periodically change the set play, calling an audible when he sees a developing opportunity.

CALLING THE TRADE

Traders have these same choices. We can be discretionary traders, placing trades based on our own subjective analysis. We can get a feel for the stock market's flow and we are able to see chart patterns as they develop. I know several highly successful discretionary traders. However, I personally prefer a systematic approach.

A systematic trader is like the quarterback who simply runs the plays as they are fed to him. Yes, I do periodically use discretion when the right opportunity develops, but I prefer to let a mathematical trading model tell me what and when to trade. This frees me of the destructive emotions that negatively affect decisions during the trading day. It also allows me to backtest various models so that I can be more certain that my approach is valid and effective.

RELATIVE STRENGTH INVESTING

The goal of relative strength investors is to buy high and sell higher. We do not try to call the bottom, preferring instead to buy into an uptrend. To use a horse racing analogy, we do not attempt to pick the winning horse before the race; we pick the horse after it runs the first straightaway. That way, we can identify the leaders.

Relative strength investing is not new. In the 1930s, analysts such as George Seaman, Robert Rhea, and Harold Gartley promoted the use of buying the strong stocks and strong industry groups. In 1965, Gilbert Haller wrote *The Haller Theory of Stock Market Trends*. His approach of constantly rotating to the best-performing stocks is the approach that many others follow, myself included. The approach gained further attention in the 1960s after Robert Levy detailed a favorable study on relative strength in *The Journal of Finance*.

There is a downside to relative strength investing—volatility. Relative strength investors typically buy securities that are more volatile than the market, and what goes up fast typically goes down even faster.

There is a theory that relative strength investing will work well in *all* market environments. During bull markets, money flows to the strongest stocks—often Nasdaq technology stocks—during bear markets, money flows to outperforming stocks, such as utilities or real estate investment trusts. Unfortunately, that theory does not work. Instead of rotating to more conservative stocks during bear markets, the approach rotates to a strong stock right before it gets clobbered. Believe me, I have first-hand experience in this!

The good news is that ETFs reduce this problem. Because ETFs hold a basket of stocks, you do not often see the scenario where an ETF defies gravity in a bear market, only to plummet once relative strength investors buy it. With ETFs, there will eventually be a rotation to more conservative securities.

To better understand the relative strength approach, let's look at two super-simple strategies that anyone can follow. (With these strategies, you only have to work one or two days a month, so they won't get in the way of your golf game!)

> *These super-simple strategies show that the concept of periodically rotating to the best-performing ETFs is a profitable approach.*

Super-Simple Strategy #1

Our first strategy rotates between broad-based equity ETFs. The ETFs we follow are iShares Large-Cap Value (IVE), Nasdaq 100 (QQQQ), SPDR S&P 500 (SPY), MidCap SPDR (MDY), iShares Small-Cap Value (IJS), iShares Small-Cap Growth (IJT), and iShares Russell 2000 (IWM). Notice that these cover the major segments of our domestic equity market.

The strategy is simple. After Friday's close, calculate a six-month percent change for each of these ETFs. Buy the two best performers. Every other week, make the same calculations again. If your holdings are one of the three best performers, then there is no trade. If, however, your ETF is not one of the top three, then sell it and buy the best performer over the prior six-month period. If you are holding the best performer, then buy the next best on the list. Do not double into an existing holding.

For our test, we calculated percent change data using a 120 business day period. This is approximately six months. For simplicity, all trades were based on Friday's closing data. A commission of $17 was factored in. The results are seen in Table 2.1.

Whereas the S&P 500, excluding dividends, was unchanged over these 12-plus years, this strategy produced an average annual rate of return of seven percent. The average holding period is 145 calendar days, so this is not a time-consuming system. The 2008 bear market was punishing, however, because the account was always fully invested and there were no conservative ETF choices.

Table 2.1: Percentage Returns for 120 Business Days

Year	ETF Trading	S&P 500 Index
1998	44.25	26.67
1999	57.85	19.53
2000	5.80	-10.14
2001	-2.23	-13.04
2002	-17.85	-23.37
2003	43.29	26.38
2004	13.01	8.99
2005	3.12	3.00
2006	8.14	13.62
2007	5.08	3.53
2008	-41.67	-38.49
2009	18.95	23.45
2010	-7.24	-5.90
AROI	7.02	0.62

Through August 31, 2010, five round-trip trades per year with an average holding period of 145 days. Past performance does not guarantee future results.

> **More Info**
> Remember that past performance does not guarantee future results. For important assumptions, see the end of this chapter.

Super-Simple Strategy #2

Super-Simple Strategy #1 took two days per month to implement. Now we will work only one day a month. Here is the strategy: at the start of each month, we calculate a one-year price change (we used 240 business days) on a list of sector ETFs. Then, we buy the two best performers to fully invest the portfolio and hold them for the remainder of the month. At the start of the next month, we run the calculations again. If a holding is not one of the two best performers, then we sell it and place the proceeds in the best performer.

The amount of sector ETFs has grown over time. For our test in 2002 we used 19 iShares sector ETFs, in 2003 we followed 24 ETFs, and in 2007 we followed 35 sector ETF choices. We could easily add many more sector ETF choices today, but for this test we capped the list at 35. Table 2.2 reveals the results.

From simply doing a monthly rotation to the best-performing ETFs over the prior year, we made seven percent annually instead of losing one percent annually in the S&P 500. Not bad for a strategy that only requires you to work one day a month!

There were great years, like the 33 percent gain in 2005 during a flat market, and there were bad years, like 2008, when the ETFs fell along with the S&P 500.

> **More Info**
> Updated performance results, the list of ETFs that we used, and the individual trades can be found at www.ETFtradingstrategies.com.

Table 2.2: Percentage Returns for 35 Sector ETFs		
Year	Sector Trading	S&P 500 Index
2002	-11.09	-23.37
2003	40.57	26.38
2004	6.31	8.99
2005	33.22	3.00
2006	20.30	13.62
2007	9.04	3.53
2008	-41.16	-38.49
2009	30.49	23.45
2010	3.20	-5.90
AROI	7.28	-1.04

Through August 31, 2010, 7.5 round-trip trades per year, with an average holding period of 98 days. Past performance does not guarantee future results.

These super-simple strategies show that the concept of periodically rotating to the best-performing ETFs is a profitable approach. That is true when we rotate once a month to the best-performing ETFs using a one-year lookback period, and it is true when we rotate every other week to the best-performing ETFs using a six-month look-back period. Nevertheless, these simple strategies can be improved. Let's take a look at the approach that we use for our managed account portfolios.

Our Relative Strength Model

Our relative strength model uses the same concept as our prior models. That is, we want to own what is doing well, and if it begins to falter, then we will sell it and rotate to a better performer. Instead of calculating a straight percentage change to measure performance, we will place greater importance on the most recent price data and place less importance on older data.

The relative strength formula breaks the past 120 business days (approximately six months) into quarters (four 30-day periods). Run a percentage change calculation on each 30-day quarter, and then average the percentage changes, placing twice the weight on the most recent quarter. The actual formula is found below.

> **Money Flow and Volume Accumulation Percent Formula Calculation**
>
> **Accumulation/Distribution Factor Calculation:**
>
> RS = ((2 x Quarter 1 Percent) + Quarter 2 Percent + Quarter 3 Percent + Quarter 4 Percent) / 5
>
> Calculating relative strength in this manner can be done with most analysis software programs.

To begin, run a six-month relative strength report that ranks a list of ETFs from best to worst based on the formula that places the most emphasis on recent price activity. Purchase the two best-performing ETFs with equal dollar amounts to establish a fully invested portfolio. Two weeks later, run the relative strength report again. If the current holdings are in the top half of the report (i.e., performing better than average), then there are no trades to be made. However, if a holding falls in the relative strength report ranking and is no longer in the top half, then sell it and purchase highest-rated ETF. Never double into a current holding.

This strategy works well on nearly any list of ETFs. To demonstrate, we will run several backtests using this approach. We will begin by running the approach on broad-based ETFs and will end this chapter with tests of sector, country, and inverse ETFs.

> **More Info**
>
> We post relative strength rankings for style, country, and sector ETFs each weekend at www.ETFtradingstrategies.com.

THE STYLE INDEX: A MARKET-DEPENDENT APPROACH

When you watch CNBC, you will notice that growth managers always say growth will outperform, value managers always say value will outperform, and small-cap managers always say small-cap stocks will outperform. Every analyst has his unique approach, and he believes his style is best. Unfortunately, market environments change. There are times when growth outperforms value and vice versa, as well as times when large caps outperform small caps and the other way around.

Instead of being locked into one trading style, it is best to employ a strategy that allows you to rotate to the best-performing market segment. That is what our Style Index program is all about.

> *The best strategy is one that allows for rotation into the market segment with the best performance.*

The first backtest of our relative strength strategy will be run on style indexes. Style indexes include large-cap growth, large-cap value, small-cap growth, small-cap value, and so forth. If you think of the Morningstar style box, we are rotating around the box, moving to those segments showing the best performance.

The largest mutual funds and ETFs are those that simply follow the S&P 500 index. Institutional investors own these because they want to "own the market." Unfortunately, the S&P 500 is a better representation of large-cap stocks than it is of the entire market. There are times when the Russell 2000, a small-cap index that holds four times as many stocks as the S&P 500, is the better performer. Why be locked into holding the S&P 500 during times when other broad-based indexes are outperforming?

The style index strategy has the flexibility to rotate to value-oriented ETFs when value is outperforming and to rotate to growth-oriented ETFs when growth is outperforming.

To develop systematic trading models, we need to be able to run backtests that cover several market cycles. That is difficult to do with ETFs because their price history is so limited. Most ETFs were introduced in 2000 or later, so running a backtest that includes the bull market of the 1990s is nearly impossible.

To get around this, we ran models on the benchmark indexes that the ETFs are designed to track during periods when the ETFs did not exist.

Here is an example—before the Nasdaq 100 ETF (QQQQ) was introduced for trading, our backtest purchased the Nasdaq 100 index. Before the iShares Small-Cap Russell 2000 Index (IWM) was introduced, the backtest bought the Russell 2000 Index. Table 2.3 details the style index ETFs that we will follow for our first test.

Table 2.3: Style Index ETF Choices

Ticker	ETF	Category
IVE	iShares Large-Cap Value	Large-cap value
QQQQ	PowerShares Nasdaq 100	Large-cap growth
SPY	SPDR S&P 500	Large-cap index
MDY	MidCap SPDRs	Mid-cap index
IJS	iShares Small-Cap Value	Small-cap value
IJT	iShares Small-Cap Growth	Small-cap growth
IWM	iShares Small-Cap Index	Small-cap index

To begin our style index rotation system using the relative strength strategy detailed earlier, a 120-day relative strength report that places most emphasis on what has happened recently is run on the ETFs in Table 2.3. At the start of the test, the two best-performing ETFs were purchased with equal dollar amounts to establish a fully invested portfolio.

Figure 2.1 shows the report on May 8, 2009. By looking at the report, you can see the S&P MidCap SPDR (MDY) and iShares S&P SmallCap 600 Value (IJS) are the two best performers, so they are purchased to create a fully invested portfolio.

Two weeks later, the relative strength report is run again. If the current holdings are in the top half of the report (i.e., one of the three best performers), then there are no trades. If a holding falls in the relative strength report ranking and is no longer in the top three, then it is sold and the highest-rated ETF is purchased. Do not double into a current holding.

Figure 2.2 shows the report on May 22, two weeks after the previous report. Notice the MidCap SPDR (MDY) remains in the top half of the report, but iShares S&P SmallCap 600 Value (IJS) is near the bottom. iShares Small-Cap Value is sold, and the proceeds enter the PowerShares Nasdaq 100 (QQQQ). This process is repeated every other week.

Figure 2.2 shows a period where a trade is made. Most weeks, however, require no trades.

For our backtest, we assume a fully invested portfolio in two ETFs. They are rebalanced to form equal positions at the end of every year. Dividends are excluded from both the ETFs' and the S&P 500's returns.

Because the ETFs follow broad market segments, this is a market-dependent system. That is, this portfolio will move in the same direction as the stock market. When holding broad-market ETFs, there is no way the portfolio will increase when the overall stock market decreases. The goal is to outperform on the way up and outperform on the way down.

Figure 2.1

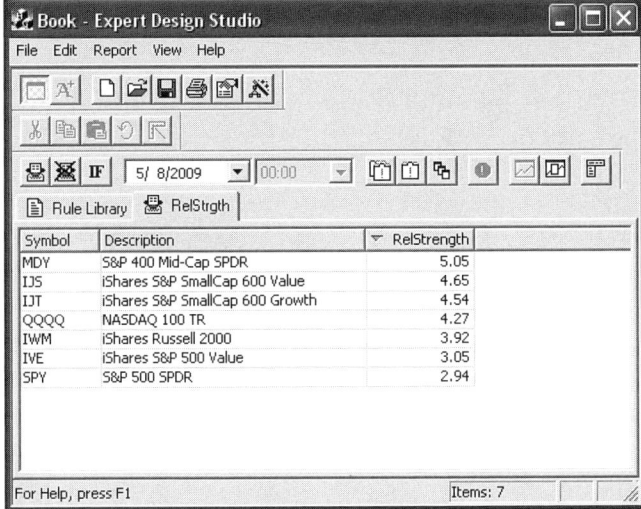

Relative Strength report shows MDY and IJS are the best performers. These become portfolio holdings.

Courtesy AIQ

Figure 2.2

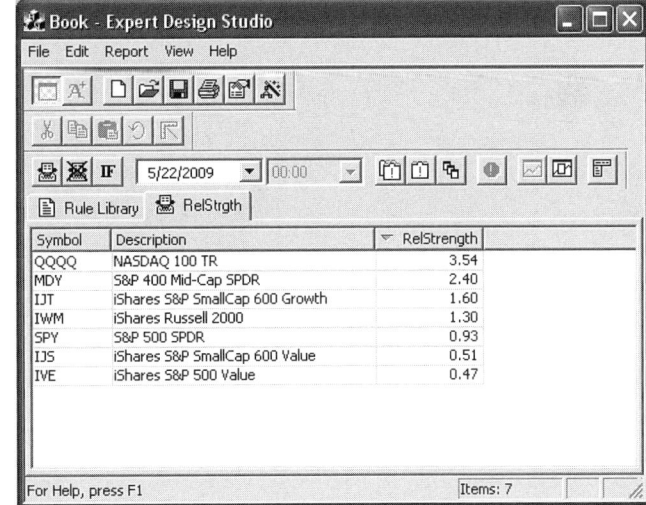

Two weeks later, IJS falls to the lower half of the report. It is sold, and the highest-ranked ETF, QQQQ, is purchased.

Courtesy AIQ

The results of this backtest are found in Table 2.4. During this nearly 13-year period, the S&P 500 was essentially flat. By being flexible enough to periodically rotate to an outperforming broad market segment, the return is well above the S&P 500 and the inflation rate.

This is an easy strategy to apply. Rotation is evaluated every other week, and in most cases, trades are not needed. Notice the average holding period is 72 calendar days.

Table 2.4: Percentage Returns Well Above S&P 500 for 13-year Period

Year	ETF Trading	S&P 500 Index
1998	41.80	26.67
1999	61.73	19.53
2000	-2.25	-10.14
2001	-3.09	-13.04
2002	-14.90	-23.37
2003	43.43	26.38
2004	12.08	8.99
2005	-1.89	3.00
2006	13.28	13.62
2007	6.77	3.53
2008	-41.00	-38.49
2009	21.29	23.45
2010	-6.20	-5.90
AROI	7.04	0.62

Through August 31, 2010, ten round-trip trades per year with an average holding period of 72 days. Past performance does not guarantee future results.

VARIATIONS

When we present this strategy to investment groups, they inevitably ask what happens when you make specific variations to the trading model. The reason for the questions is that they want to tweak the system to fit their own trading needs. They want to become more comfortable with the model.

While we have already detailed a successful approach, readers may prefer one of the variations to the model. Those who are uncomfortable waiting two weeks to evaluate a trade might prefer Variation #1, while those who want to limit drawdowns may choose Variation #2. We present several variations here in hopes of answering the specific questions you may have on the model.

Table 2.5: Yearly Backtest Results Similar to Table 2.4, with Increase in Number of Trades

Year	ETF Trading	S&P 500 Index
1998	40.06	26.67
1999	57.74	19.53
2000	2.19	-10.14
2001	0.36	-13.04
2002	-16.69	-23.37
2003	41.84	26.38
2004	15.04	8.99
2005	2.60	3.00
2006	12.71	13.62
2007	3.92	3.53
2008	-40.09	-38.49
2009	20.69	23.45
2010	-5.51	-5.90
AROI	7.60	0.62

Through August 31, 2010, 12.4 round-trip trades per year with an average holding period of 58 days. Past performance does not guarantee future results.

Variation #1: Rotate Every Week

In our first variation, we will evaluate the relative strength report every week (as opposed to every other week) to look for possible rotation opportunities. Except for this variation, the methodology outline in the previous section applies.

Table 2.5 shows the yearly backtest results. The yearly returns are very similar to the previous returns, but the number of trades increased. Slippage would lower the overall return.

I am not willing to trade more if the system does not get you in earlier in an uptrend and out earlier in a downtrend. While this variation may be a better fit for some of our readers—those that want more active trading and are uncomfortable evaluating their holdings every other week—I myself am not willing to increase the trading for close to the same overall return.

Variation #2: Adding a Bond Fund

The next variation to the style index approach is to add a bond fund to the ETF choices found in Table 2.3. Because no ETF bond fund dates back to 1997, we used the Vanguard Long-Term U.S. Bond (VUSTX) mutual fund as a proxy. It is reasonable to assume that a bond ETF, like the iShares 20+ U.S. Treasury Bond (TLT), would have similar movement. Beginning in 2009, we used TLT instead of the Vanguard mutual fund.

We used the same trading methodology as the style index strategy, with one exception—by adding a bond fund, there were eight ETF choices. Our goal is to own ETFs in the top half of the report, so as long as the current holdings are in the top four positions of the relative strength report, then there are no trades (as opposed to the top three positions in the original style index approach).

The results of our backtest are found in Table 2.6. While the overall return is about the same as the style index return, the portfolio met its goal of outperforming on the way up and outperforming on the way down. By rotating half the portfolio to a bond fund during the bear markets of 2000 through 2003 and then again in 2008, the drawdowns were less than the

S&P 500. During the bull years, the portfolio rose more than the S&P 500. That is especially true in 1999 and 2003.

Adding a bond fund may limit drawdowns and allow the portfolio to outperform on the way up as well as on the way down.

Table 2.6: Adding a Bond Fund Limits Effects of Drawdowns

Year	ETF Trading	S&P 500 Index
1998	33.18	26.67
1999	57.41	19.53
2000	5.34	-10.14
2001	3.35	-13.04
2002	-12.91	-23.37
2003	34.81	26.38
2004	10.65	8.99
2005	-0.74	3.00
2006	8.96	13.62
2007	6.43	3.53
2008	-31.58	-38.49
2009	18.98	23.45
2010	6.19	-5.90
AROI	8.91	0.62

Through August 31, 2010, seven round-trip trades per year with an average holding period of 102 days. Past performance does not guarantee future results.

Variation #3: Adding International Funds (Style Index Portfolios)

The style index strategy rotates to broad market segments, such as large-cap growth or small-cap value. In keeping with this concept, it would not make sense to add specific countries. Adding broad international choices, however, fits the approach. For this variation, we will take the ETF choices found in Table 2.3, but we will add two broad-based international funds: iShares International Emerging Markets (EEM) and iShares EAFE International Developed Markets (EFA).

That means our strategy rotates between nine ETF choices, so we want to hold ETFs in the top four positions of the report (remember, we want our holdings to be in the top half of the report). If, during a rotation period, a current holding falls below the top four positions on the relative strength report, then that holding is switched to the ETF showing the highest relative strength.

The testing results are found in Table 2.7. Adding two international choices greatly improved results. There are many years—such as 1998, 1999, 2003, and 2007—where the strategy's advance far outpaced that of the S&P 500. What goes up faster than the market typically falls faster than the market when the market turns south, but that is not the case in this situation. The trading portfolio fell less than the market between 2000 and 2003 because the strategy rotated to the better-performing small-cap arena. In 2008, the strategy was only slightly worse than a buy-and-hold approach.

During the entire testing period, the S&P 500 was essentially unchanged. By periodically placing a trade using broad-based ETF choices, the average annual rate of return was 11 percent. That means this paper portfolio doubled its value in eight years!

In our backtest, we assumed the portfolio was always fully invested. For those who would like to incorporate market timing, the strategy works well because it only takes one sell order to move the portfolio to 50 percent cash. The backtested return, however, shows that market timing is not necessary when there is good security selection.

This is not an active trading strategy. Notice the average holding period is 109 calendar days. With the additional ETF choices, the portfolio holdings had a bit more room to fluctuate on the relative strength report and the number of whipsaw trades was reduced.

Because of the emerging market ETF addition, portfolio volatility was increased under this variation. Still, for most people, adding international ETF choices is a good idea. This is the approach that I employ for the clients in my Style Index Portfolios managed account program online at www.ETFportfolios.net.

Table 2.7: Adding International Funds Increases Returns

Year	ETF Trading	S&P 500 Index
1998	41.60	26.67
1999	54.92	19.53
2000	5.28	-10.14
2001	1.49	-13.04
2002	-15.26	-23.37
2003	49.40	26.38
2004	14.38	8.99
2005	11.68	3.00
2006	15.29	13.62
2007	20.80	3.53
2008	-42.13	-38.49
2009	30.55	23.45
2010	-3.67	-5.90
AROI	11.22	0.62

Through August 31, 2010, 6.3 round-trip trades per year with an average holding of 109 days. Past performance does not guarantee future returns.

> **More Info**
> For details on every transaction and updated performance statistics, visit www.ETFtradingstrategies.com.

SECTOR TRADING: A (SOMEWHAT) MARKET-INDEPENDENT APPROACH

The style index rotation model traded broad market segments, such as large-cap, small-cap, growth, or value. A more aggressive approach is to trade sector ETFs. Examples of sector ETFs are funds related to banking, semiconductors, and health care. They are less diversified and offer a higher profit potential than the style indexes.

For a long time, I worked under the assumption that in every market environment there would be a sector doing well. In a bull market, that sector is often related to technology. In a bear market, the strongest sector may be utilities or gold. For me, a lesson of the 2008 bear market was that there are times when all sectors fall.

That is why sector investing is "somewhat" market independent—it works best in bull markets, but the approach does have a chance to increase in bearish markets as well. During the worst bear markets, however, sector rotation portfolios will fall.

Backtesting a trading strategy for sector ETFs is even harder than testing the style index ETFs, because sector ETFs began trading in the early 2000s, but there was not a broad list until around 2005, and new sector ETFs are still being introduced today.

Fortunately, sector mutual funds, such as those from Fidelity Investments, have more history, and models can be run on these funds. If a model works on Fidelity sector funds, it should work on sector ETFs as well.

> *Trading sector ETFs is a more aggressive strategy because they are less diversified and offer a higher profit potential than the style indexes.*

Table 2.8: Sector Rotation Backtest with Exceptional Results		
Year	ETF Trading	S&P 500 Index
1998	30.25	26.67
1999	93.77	19.53
2000	39.88	-10.14
2001	-7.65	-13.04
2002	-14.10	-23.37
2003	35.20	26.38
2004	26.35	8.99
2005	25.47	3.00
2006	14.05	13.62
2007	16.11	3.53
2008	-36.80	-38.49
2009	55.47	23.45
2010	4.07	-5.90
AROI	17.97	0.62

Through August 31, 2010; four round-trip trades per year with an average holding period of 184 days. Past performance does not guarantee future results.

Fidelity Sector Funds

Fidelity Investments allowed traders to profit from sector rotation when it launched its sector mutual funds in the 1980s. It catered to traders by offering hourly pricing on these Select Sector funds.

We ran our relative strength model on 41 sector funds from the Fidelity mutual fund family. As explained earlier, our trading strategy uses a relative strength calculation that breaks the last 120 trading days into quarters and calculates a percentage return figure for each. These returns are then averaged, placing twice the weight on the most recent quarter's worth of data.

At the start of the test, the two highest-ranked Fidelity sector funds were purchased with equal dollar amounts to establish a fully invested portfolio. Two weeks later, the same relative strength report was run again. If the current holdings were rated in the top half of the report (i.e., in the top 20), then there were no trades. If a holding fell out of the top half in the relative strength report, it was sold and the highest-rated sector fund was purchased. The portfolio was always fully invested in two sector funds.

In our backtest, the buy and sell prices used were the closing prices at the end of the week (i.e., the day the reports were run). In actual trading, trades would occur on the following business day. Also, the portfolio was rebalanced at the end of each year to create equal positions in the two holdings.

The strategy is designed to rotate to the sectors of the market that have the best performance. In this case, the results are exceptional (see Table 2.8). Our strategy outperformed each year. The 40 percent return in 2000, a year the market fell, is especially impressive. That year, the strategy benefited from the technology run at the start of 2000, but rotated out of technology before the year was finished.

I published this strategy in 2003 and have followed it ever since. Although we are showing a backtest, it has actually been a walk-forward paper portfolio since that time. In 2003, I was obviously impressed with the returns, but I thought the portfolio would be crushed someday because of its aggressive nature. After all, a fully invested portfolio only holds two sector funds. Amazingly, it has continued to perform consistently well, showing that the model is sound. Because of its aggressive nature, this approach should only be a small portion of anyone's assets. Risk can be lowered by holding more than two securities in the portfolio.

Sector ETFs

Our relative strength model works for Fidelity sector funds. How does it work on ETFs? The iShares family offers the most sector funds, so we used these funds for our test. Sector ETFs began trading in 2001, so our test began in 2002. In addition to traditional sectors, we also included four in-

Table 2.9: Sector and International Region ETFs Used in Sector Backtest

2002:	2003-06:	2007-10:
ICF	ICF	ICF
IYM	IYM	IYM
IYC	IYC	IYC
IYK	IYK	IYK
IYE	IYE	IYE
IYF	IYF	IYF
IYG	IYG	IYG
IYH	IYH	IYH
IYJ	IYJ	IYJ
IYR	IYR	IYR
IYW	IYW	IYW
IYZ	IYZ	IYZ
IDU	IDU	IDU
IGE	IGE	IGE
IGN	IGN	IGN
IGW	IGW	IGW
IGV	IGV	IGV
IGM	IGM	IGM
IBB	IBB	IBB
	EZU	EZU
	IEV	IEV
	EPP	EPP
	ITF	ITF
	ILF	ILF
		IEZ
		IHF
		IHE
		IEO
		ITA
		IHI
		IAK
		IAI
		IYT
		IAT
		ITB

ternational region ETFs. Most of these ETFs began in 2002, so they were included in our backtest at the start of 2003. In 2003, we used 24 sector ETFs. In 2007, we added new ETFs, bringing the list to 35 choices. Although we could and should add more choices, we have kept the list at 35, as you can see in Table 2.9.

As before, the buy and sell prices used were the closing prices at the end of the week (i.e., the day the reports were run). In actual trading, trades would occur near the next day's opening price. A $17 commission was factored in.

Also, the portfolio was rebalanced at the end of each year to create equal positions in the two holdings. Dividends were not factored in.

The results can be found in Table 2.10. There were not enough sector choices to avoid the down years of 2002 and 2008, but there were some great years, such as 2005, where the portfolio had an exceptional return in what was a flat market. Energy and natural resources holdings were instrumental that year. The year 2003 was huge because networking doubled in value and a semiconductor holding leaped 27 percent.

The results, however, were less than the Fidelity sector fund returns. Adding more sector ETF choices, especially from other ETF families, would help.

In other cases, Fidelity offers funds that ETFs do not offer. For example, the Fidelity sector fund portfolio had an impressive 47 percent return in 2009 because of an automotive holding (auto bailouts and the cash-for-clunkers program were good for auto stocks!). A similar ETF choice does not exist. With the advent of more specialized ETFs, this discrepancy will reduce over time.

> **More Info**
>
> For details on every transaction and updated performance statistics, visit www.ETFtradingstrategies.com.

Table 2.10: Sector ETF Rotation Backtest with Results Less than Fidelity Sector Fund Returns

Year	Sector Trading	S&P 500 Index
2002	-25.43	-23.37
2003	82.73	26.38
2004	6.26	8.99
2005	35.74	3.00
2006	21.52	13.62
2007	40.48	3.53
2008	-36.97	-38.49
2009	20.72	23.45
2010	-7.41	-5.90
AROI	10.42	-1.04

Through August 31, 2010, 4.4 round-trip trades with an average holding period of 165 days. Past performance does not guarantee future results.

TACTICAL ALLOCATION: A MARKET-INDEPENDENT APPROACH

When I wrote *ETF Trading Strategies Revealed* in 2006, there were no inverse funds. During bearish market environments, my hope was that there would be one or two sectors that bucked the market's downtrend. We now know that inverse funds must be used to have a market-independent, or all-weather, approach.

Inverse funds have problems. They may not follow their market indexes the way we would like them to. For me, this is not a big concern—I just want them to rise in value when I own them. To run a portfolio that can do well in any market environment, inverse funds—warts and all—need to play an integral role.

> *Inverse funds will play an integral role in any trading strategy intended to perform well in all market environments.*

After managing the Style Index Portfolio for seven years, I have learned that limiting the rotation model to a small set of ETFs is beneficial to quick rotation. Sometimes less is more. Instead of adding some inverse ETFs to a large list of sector and international ETFs, I will instead limit my choices to just a few market segments. That allows for quicker rotation between the segments as the market environment changes.

To this point, all of our tests have used two ETFs as a fully invested portfolio. That is fine for the style index choices, but holding only market-segment ETFs in a portfolio is extremely aggressive. For our first test, we will reduce the risk by holding three ETFs in a fully invested portfolio.

Three-ETF Test

Table 2.11 shows the ETFs we tracked for this test. Notice that at least two ETFs work well in any market environment. When equities are bullish, the SPDR S&P 500, Nasdaq 100, and possibly the Emerging Markets rise to the top of the report. When equities are bearish, the inverse S&P 500 rises to the top of the report. In any environment, either the bullish dollar or bearish dollar should be increasing.

As is the case for earlier tests, many of these ETFs have little price history. To perform a better backtest, we used the indexes that the ETFs track. So before the PowerShares commodity ETF was traded, we bought and sold a commodity index.

It was even more difficult to get data for the inverse funds. To create price history for these instruments, we used the underlying index and built an index based on their daily percentage moves. In other words, if the S&P 500 increased by 0.6 percent on a given day, then our created index decreased by 0.6 percent.

Table 2.11: ETF Choices for Three-ETF Tests

Ticker	ETF	Category
UDN	PowerShares Bearish Dollar	Inverse U.S. dollar
UUP	PowerShares Bullish Dollar	Bullish U.S. dollar
TLT	iShares 20+ Year Treasury	U.S. Treasury
SPY	SPDR S&P 500	Large-cap index
SH	ProShares Short S&P 500	Inverse large-cap index
QQQQ	PowerShares QQQQ	Nasdaq 100
DBC	PowerShares Commodities	Commodities
EEM	iShares Emerging Mkts	Emerging international markets

Obviously, results would be different if there was actual price history on these ETFs. So we are not saying what a portfolio would have done; we simply want to see if this strategy is sound and if it can be applied to real money as we move forward.

As before, the ETFs were bought and sold using Friday's closing price the day of the signal. A $15 commission was applied. Since we have eight ETF choices, our relative strength model holds the ETFs in the top four positions.

The yearly percentage results are found in Table 2.12. A graph of portfolio returns is found in Figure 2.3, where the top line represents the backtested portfolio and the bottom line represents the S&P 500.

Table 2.12: Yearly Percentage Results for Market-independent Strategy		
Year	Sector Trading	S&P 500 Index
1998	24.48	26.67
1999	51.06	19.53
2000	-2.36	-10.14
2001	-2.34	-13.04
2002	-4.75	-23.37
2003	36.60	26.38
2004	9.38	8.99
2005	6.73	3.00
2006	5.76	13.62
2007	21.62	3.53
2008	13.67	-38.49
2009	30.12	23.45
2010	-4.04	-5.90
AROI	13.48	0.62

Through August 31, 2010, Ten round-trip trades per year with an average holding period of 113 days. Largest drawdown: 18 percent from March 9, 2000 to April 16, 2000. This does not represent the returns a portfolio would have achieved. It is simply to determine if the trading strategy is sound. Past performance does not guarantee future results.

Figure 2.3

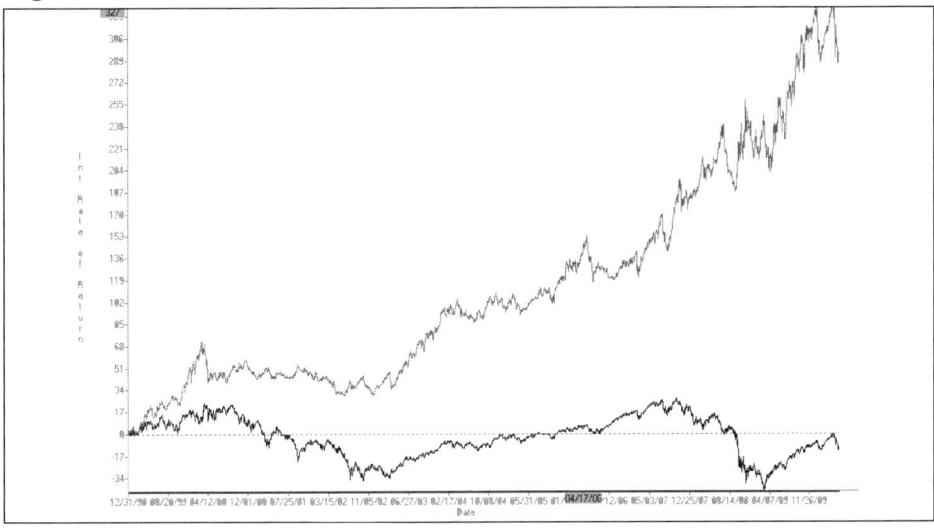

The graph shows portfolio return (upper line) versus the S&P 500 (lower line) for the market-independent approach using three ETF holdings. | Courtesy AIQ

> **More Info**
>
> For details on every transaction and updated performance statistics, visit www.ETFtradingstrategies.com.

We were very pleased with the results. The portfolio lost money during the 2000 through 2002 bear market, but it did not lose much. It achieved its market-independent goal in 2008 by gaining 13.7 percent during a time that the S&P 500 lost 38 percent.

As we ran our backtest and hand-entered the trades, we found that there was excessive trading. It is not an active strategy (generally one round-trip trade per month), but there were more trades than necessary. Generally, there were one or two big winners and the third position kept rotating in and out of securities with little to show for it. When it comes to broad ETFs like those in our list, two holdings may be fine.

Tactical Allocation Portfolio

Our final and most effective market-independent approach uses a small variation from the previous test. Instead of using three ETFs for a fully invested portfolio, we will say that using two ETFs is fully invested. That increases risk, as half of the portfolio will be short the market during certain periods. We will also remove the long U.S. dollar ETF choice from our list of ETFs (after all, we Americans are long the dollar anyway!). Table 2.13 shows the list of ETFs that we track.

Table 2.13: Tactical Allocation ETF Choices

Ticker	ETF	Category
UDN	PowerShares Bearish Dollar	Inverse U.S. dollar
TLT	iShares 20+ Year Treasury	U.S. Treasury
SPY	SPDR S&P 500	Large-cap index
SH	ProShares Short S&P 500	Inverse large-cap index
QQQQ	PowerShares QQQQ	Nasdaq 100
DBC	PowerShares Commodities	Commodities
EEM	iShares Emerging Markets	Emerging international markets

In running this backtest, our goal is not to see how well a portfolio would have performed—after all, we have had to create mock indexes to represent the inverse funds and to trade market indexes before the ETFs existed. Our goal is to see if the strategy is sound and whether it would be appropriate to apply funds to the strategy as we move forward.

Using our relative strength strategy highlighted at the beginning of this chapter, we buy the top-ranked ETFs and hold them as long as they are in the top three. Because there are so few ETF choices, the rotation is quicker. This is a case where less is more.

At the start of the backtest, we purchased the two highest-ranked ETFs using the relative strength formula that weighs recent price activity more

Figure 2.4

The relative strength report favors a short S&P 500 position and a bond position on September 26, 2008.

Courtesy AIQ

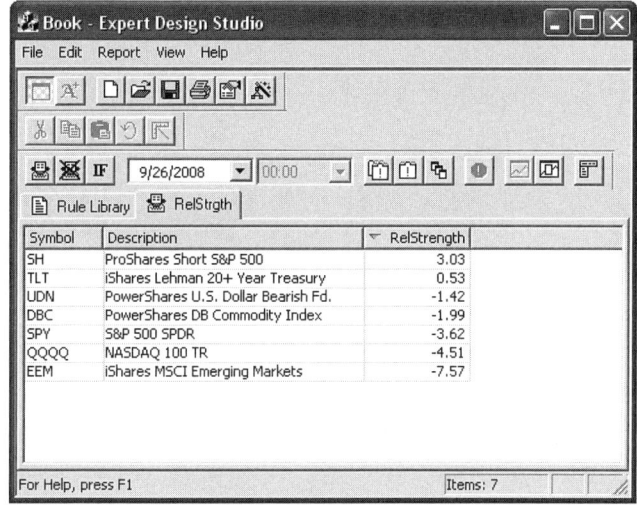

Figure 2.5

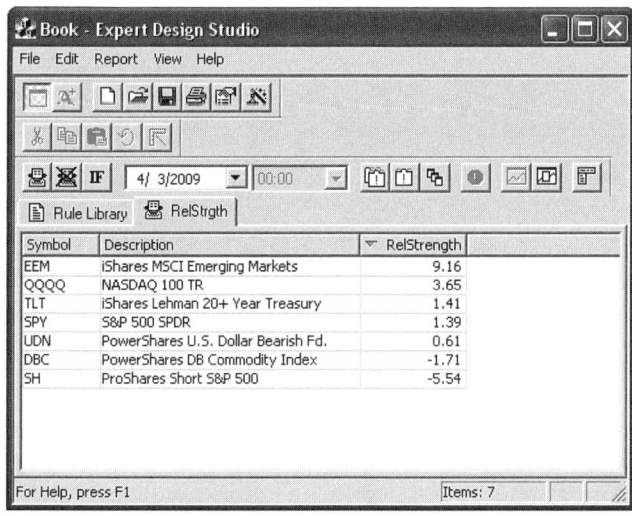

The relative strength report favors emerging markets and the Nasdaq 100 on April 3, 2009.

Courtesy AIQ

Mechanical Trading Models   41

Table 2.14: Tactical Allocation Percentage Returns

Year	ETF Trading	S&P 500 Index
1998	22.64	26.67
1999	59.16	19.53
2000	3.59	-10.14
2001	2.85	-13.04
2002	-3.21	-23.37
2003	38.98	26.38
2004	15.80	8.99
2005	15.00	3.00
2006	4.01	13.62
2007	19.35	3.53
2008	16.06	-38.49
2009	35.78	23.45
2010	0.53	-5.90
AROI	17.01	0.62

Through August 31, 2010, 6.3 round-trip trades per year with an average holding period of 118 days. The largest drawdowns included 21 percent from March 7, 2000 to April 16, 2000; 20 percent from July 15, 2008 to September 19, 2008; 16 percent from May 11, 2006 to June 14, 2006. This does not represent the returns a portfolio would have achieved. It is simply to determine whether the trading strategy is sound. Past performance does not guarantee future results.

than the activity from six months ago. Two weeks later, the relative strength report was run again. If portfolio holdings were ranked in the top three, then there were no trades. If a holding fell below the top three, it was sold and the top position was purchased. We never double into a fund.

To get a feel for how this works, Figure 2.4 shows the relative strength report on September 26, 2008. This is right before the most severe plunge during the 2008 bear market. Notice that the short S&P 500 and the bond ETF are at the top of the ranking. Then on April 3, 2009, shortly after the market reached an important low, the system favored the highly aggressive emerging markets and Nasdaq 100 ETFs (see Figure 2.5). The system does not call the tops and bottoms, but it catches the major trends.

A $15 commission was included, and Friday's closing prices were used for each trade. In actual trading, trades would be placed on the following Monday.

Table 2.14 shows the portfolio return. Limiting our portfolio to two ETFs truly made this a market-independent approach. In the nearly 13-year test,

Figure 2.6

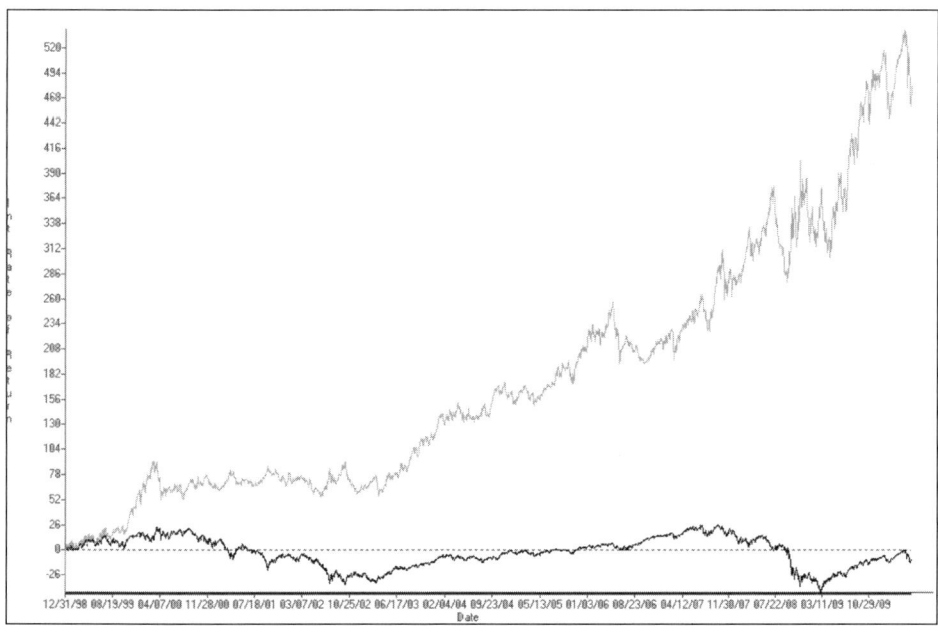

The graph shows portfolio return (upper line) versus the S&P 500 (lower line) for the market Tactical Allocation approach using two ETF holdings. | Courtesy AIQ

there was only one down year, and that down year only lost three percent! A graph of returns is found in Figure 2.6. Needless to say, we are extremely pleased with the results. The effectiveness of this strategy demonstrates the importance of ETFs and how they benefit today's investor. Although relative strength investing has a long history, investors could not have followed a market-independent strategy such as this without going to the futures market or shorting securities. Finally, a market-independent approach is available to every investor!

CHOICES WITH ETFS

With ETFs, we can easily rotate to long equities, short equities, commodities, currencies (i.e., short dollar), or international markets. Early in an ETF's growth cycle, new choices may emerge, while some may also be removed. As I write this, securities regulators are examining whether commodity ETFs are becoming too big for the marketplace. The key takeaway is to have a small set of ETFs that represent different market segments. The more they move independently of one another, the better.

The ETF list should be small, but it is important that there is at least one ETF that does well—that is the key to the strategy. In 2010, the iShares 20+ Year Treasury (TLT) was the winner. By removing that selection, or by following the PowerShares Inverse U.S. Treasury (TBT) instead, results would be far worse. Without TLT, there were no big winning trades and one of the portfolio holdings was often on the wrong side of what was a trendless market.

The tactical allocation ETF list in Table 2.13 was not chosen randomly. These funds are all very liquid. In a good equity market, the S&P 500 SPDR, the QQQQ, and maybe the emerging markets ETFs will do well. In a bad equity market, the inverse S&P 500 will do well. The other half of the portfolio will likely reside in the Treasury bond ETF or the bearish dollar ETF.

There are ways to increase the returns during bullish markets. When the model calls for a holding in the S&P 500, aggressive investors may choose to own the ProShares Ultra S&P 500 (SSO). This moves twice as fast as the S&P 500.

Another approach to boost returns during bullish periods is to use a modified top-down approach. When the system favors equity index holdings (i.e., the S&P 500 and Nasdaq 100), aggressive investors can run the relative strength report on a list of sector ETFs and buy the strongest sectors. Along the same lines, if the market favors international markets (i.e., emerging markets), the relative strength report can be run on a list of international ETFs and the top two countries can be purchased.

Once the system rotates out of equities or international markets, the sector or country ETFs would be sold. Just as top-down investors would not want to hold a good stock in a weak group, we should not hold a sector ETF when the model is out of equities, and we should not hold a country ETF when the model is out of the international markets.

When doesn't the model work well? Sideways markets are difficult. Remember, the key to the strategy is making sure that there is always an ETF that is in an uptrend. So if the equity market is going nowhere, then it is important that there is an uptrending ETF outside of the equity arena, such as long or short bonds, that is being tracked. Having a temporary spike in a security also causes problems for this model. Long and steady trends are preferred.

Having a portion of one's portfolio in a market-independent strategy makes sense. I have tried trading inverse ETFs based on judgment, but doing so is stressful and requires constant analysis—and is very hard to do in some market environments. The fact that the model tests well and is fully mechanical is appealing. It is so appealing that I am adding this as a portfolio option for my managed account program.

RELATIVE STRENGTH CONCLUSIONS

There is an old joke: "Put two economists in a room and you will get three opinions." The same is true for investment analysts. Log on to CNBC.com, and you will see articles proclaiming that the market is heading significantly higher, as well as articles stating that the market is heading for a freefall. Notice, however, that one's opinion of the market does not matter in our relative strength trading model. We do not tell the market what it should do—that is dangerous and can lead us to be wrong for long periods of time. Instead, it is the market that tells *us* what to do.

> *One's opinion of the market does not matter; rather, the market tells one what to do.*

We used a relative rotation strategy with a one-year look-back period, a six-month look-back period, and a customized look-back formula. They all worked; there is no magical look-back period. Instead, it is the concept of the system—that one wants to own the market leaders—that is important.

We applied our customized relative strength trading model, a model I have used since 2003 for client portfolios, to many sets of ETFs. The model worked for style index ETFs, sector ETFs, Fidelity sector funds, and market-segment ETFs, including inverse choices.

The fact that the model worked for many sets of ETFs is reassuring. If it worked for only one set of ETFs and not others, then I would lose confidence. Readers can use the model on whichever ETF list they prefer.

It is also reassuring to know that the model is simple. Steve Palmquist, author of *Money-Making Candlestick Patterns: Backtested for Proven Results* as well as a good friend of mine, says that if you cannot explain a trading model to a child, then you should not use it. Complicated and over-optimized models work for short periods of time, but then they lose their effectiveness and fade away. Our model is based on the simple belief that there will always be an area of the market that is outperforming, and that we will benefit by rotating to that area.

> **More Info**
> For those who cannot run their own calculations, we post weekly relative strength rankings on the Analysis page of www.ETFtradingstrategies.com.

ASSUMPTIONS

In this chapter, we have examined several different strategies for portfolio growth through the lens of backtesting. Backtesting historical data is an effective method for determining whether or not a strategy is useful. One should never put real money into a system that has a poor backtest result. Our backtests were not intended to indicate the returns of a portfolio. Instead, we are analyzing past performance of benchmark indexes and user-created indexes to test a rotation strategy for ETFs, even though the ETFs are a relatively new investment vehicle.

There are many assumptions to our tests. The backtests assumed the portfolio was always fully invested. Many of the ETFs were not yet available to purchase at the beginning date of the backtest. In this case, the backtest used the ETF's benchmark index as a substitute and used price data from the actual ETFs once they became available. Studies show a high, but not exact, correlation between the benchmark indexes and the ETFs.

For inverse ETF data, we inverted the daily percentage change figures from the underlying index to create our own inverse data. Needless to say, the price data from an inverse ETF would be different. We used actual inverse ETF data once they were available.

The percentage returns represent a hypothetical backtest instead of actual performance. The backtest's returns and other figures have not been audited, but are based upon information obtained from public sources believed to be reliable. Since no funds were managed using the strategies during this period, the impact that economic and market factors might have had on the trading cannot be represented.

The strategies were run with a view toward capital appreciation with risk levels higher than the S&P 500. Because of turnover rates, portfolios are subject to higher tax costs than portfolios with lesser turnover.

Dividends and interest payments were excluded from the data. Trades were placed on Friday's closing prices, even though a real portfolio would place trades on the following Monday. Slippage is not included.

As with any strategy, past performance does not guarantee future results or that losses will not occur.

FINAL THOUGHTS

We have highlighted aggressive growth portfolios that may be appropriate for a portion of one's overall investment portfolio. Many people buy and hold an S&P 500 index fund or an equity mutual fund. They may be better served by utilizing the style index approach. More aggressive investors may choose the sector rotation model. Finally, the tactical allocation program is appropriate for those who do not want to rely on a long-term uptrending market to achieve their investment goals.

We began this chapter with a football analogy, comparing mechanical trading to a quarterback who runs plays called from his coaching staff. Sometimes, the plays work well and the team drives toward the end zone. At other times, the opposition has the momentum. The same holds true for trading mechanical systems.

Our backtests show nice profits nearly every year, but that does not mean trading is easy. Within each year, there were periods where the trades turned into losses. There were periods where the market zigged when the mechanical model zagged. The best quarterbacks, like Joe Montana and Tom Brady, stay calm when the game is not going as expected and they do not deviate from the game plan.

Similarly, the advantage of mechanical models is that they take human emotion out of the decision making process. Mechanical traders should remain calm when things are not going well and they should stick to the game plan. Moving forward, a trader's real portfolio should resemble the returns from paper trading the mechanical model. That way he or she is more likely to achieve the success the mechanical model provides.

Some may be able to apply discretionary methods, such as interpreting chart patterns for better entry and exit executions, to improve on the mechanical model. That is what Chapter 3 is all about.

Quick Quiz

1) Relative strength models attempt to _____.

   a. buy low and sell high.

   b. buy high and sell higher.

2) When it comes to sector investing, there is always a bull market somewhere.

   a. True

   b. False

3) Which of the following is not true about the Tactical Allocation Model?

   a. The model only works as an "all-weather" portfolio as long as there is an ETF choice that will benefit from any market environment.

   b. The model attempts to call tops and bottoms in securities.

   c. The model benefits from trendless markets by buying oversold conditions and selling overbought conditions.

For the answers to this quiz, please visit the Trader's Library Education Corner online at www.TradersLibrary.com/TLEcorner.

3 Adding Insightful Chart Pattern Analysis

There are many advantages to running trading systems with computer models. For example, a computer can give buy and sell signals without the emotional baggage that human judgment brings. There is one type of analysis that a computer cannot be programmed to do well, however—and that is chart pattern analysis. By knowing a handful of chart patterns, you can apply insightful analysis in addition to the work performed by quantitative models.

An advantage of chart pattern analysis is that it is always valid. Many mechanical trading systems and indicator readings gain and lose their effectiveness over time, but proper chart analysis remains consistent. Chart pattern analysis is subjective, however, so practice helps to achieve reliability.

Chart patterns do not call exact market tops or bottoms. In each chart, the analyst waits for a sign, such as a trend line break, that indicates that a trend has actually reversed. Instead of calling tops or bottoms, chart pattern analysis gives an early indication as to when a new trend has emerged.

Some of the most successful traders I know use only chart pattern analysis. I use it too, but not to the degree that some others do. Some people are better at this form of analysis than others—some people have a gift for it, while others find it more challenging. Nevertheless, there are some simple patterns that all agree are valuable. The patterns we will cover are the rectangle, right triangle, symmetrical triangle, and wedge.

Chart pattern analysis is always valid.

RECTANGLE PATTERN

A rectangle pattern is formed when a security fluctuates back and forth in a narrow range. One horizontal line is drawn connecting the highs and another horizontal line is drawn connecting the lows. The upper trend line represents resistance, and the lower trend line represents support.

The more times a trend line is touched and a reversal occurs, the more powerful its support or resistance becomes. When a rectangle pattern is forming, the security is often said to be consolidating, or in a trading range.

The direction of the breakout from this pattern cannot be predicted. On the bet that the pattern will continue intact, short-term traders can enter long positions when the security is near its lower support line and enter short positions when the security is near its upper resistance line. Stops are placed just outside the pattern.

Figure 3.1

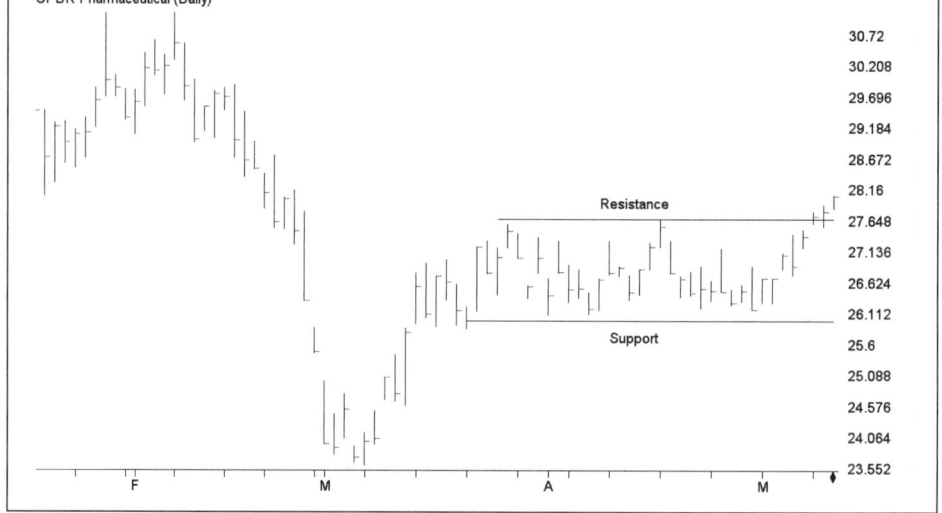

A rectangle pattern in the SPDR Pharmaceuticals ETF (XPH). | Courtesy AIQ

Most traders, however, wait for the eventual breakout from the pattern, which is most often in the direction of the longer-term trend. Typically, the longer the security remains in the pattern, the bigger the move after the breakout. Ideally, the breakout comes with heavy volume (more details on ETF volume appear in Chapter 5: Technical Indicators).

Figure 3.1 shows a daily chart of the SPDR Pharmaceutical (XPH). For nearly two months, this ETF moved in a narrow range. Buyers emerged when its price approached $26 and sellers emerged when the price approached $27.60. Trend lines were drawn at the upper and lower extremes of the price range; the upper trend line represents resistance, and the lower trend line represents support.

While in the trading range, one does not know whether support or resistance will be broken. Wait for the breakout, which happened on the right side of the chart in Figure 3.1. Ideally, when the break occurs, you want the ETF to close near the high of its daily price bar. That is what happened on the chart's last price bar.

Since this is an ETF instead of a stock, the break above resistance implies that several of the stocks within its index also consolidated and were performing well at the time of the break.

Typically, the longer the security remains in the pattern, the bigger the move after the breakout.

RIGHT TRIANGLE PATTERN

The right triangle is a pattern that exhibits a series of narrower price fluctuations. On one side of the fluctuation, the boundary of price action is horizontal. The boundary on the other side slopes toward the opposite (horizontal) boundary. An ascending triangle (also known as a right triangle) has a horizontal top and an ascending bottom; a descending triangle is the reverse.

In most cases, it is the horizontal trend line that is broken in this pattern. Therefore, caution should be exercised when a descending triangle is developing. Likewise, be ready to buy long when an ascending triangle is developing.

If the security breaks the sloping trend line instead of the horizontal trend line, then the resulting move has less significance. If the downward-sloping trend line on a descending triangle is broken, the security may only rally to its previous reaction high.

A good example of this type of action is found in Figure 3.2. In this chart, the British Pound's horizontal support of $194 was tested on several occasions from February through June. During this period, each rally was less than the previous rally. Because this is a descending triangle, it suggests the eventual break would be to the downside. In this case, however, the sloping line was broken. The resulting move was small. In August, the more important horizontal trend line was broken and a downtrend emerged. A break of a horizontal trend line, especially if it has been tested on more than two occasions, is more significant than a break of a sloping trend line.

Figure 3.2

A right triangle pattern in CurrencyShares British Pound (FXB). | Courtesy AIQ

SYMMETRICAL TRIANGLE PATTERN

Whereas the right triangle has one horizontal trend line and one sloping trend line, the symmetrical triangle has two sloping trend lines that form two sides of the triangle. Because the trend lines slope in opposite directions, they intersect somewhere around the middle of the existing price range—that is, the price fluctuates up and down, but each move is smaller than its predecessor.

The descending tops in the price movement are defined by a downward-sloping boundary line (resistance line), and the low points in the fluctuation are defined by an upward-sloping line (support line). The upper and lower lines need not be of equal length.

Figure 3.3 shows a nice example of a symmetrical triangle. Notice each rally in iShares MSCI Taiwan (EWT) is weaker than the previous rally and each decline is milder than the previous decline. Volatility decreases throughout the pattern. When the break comes, volatility increases.

Figure 3.3

A symmetrical triangle pattern in iShares MSCI Taiwan (EWT). | Courtesy AIQ

Adding Insightful Chart Pattern Analysis

The symmetrical triangle occurs less often than the previous patterns discussed. Although I have not quantified this statement, I believe this pattern is less effective than the rectangle or right triangle patterns. Nevertheless, it shows the important concept that periods of high volatility typically precede periods of low volatility.

> *Periods of high volatility typically precede periods of low volatility.*

WEDGE PATTERN

A wedge is similar to the symmetrical triangle, except the entire wedge slants in an upward or downward direction. The range of daily prices narrows as the price enters the wedge's intersection. A falling wedge is typically a bullish pattern, so a break above its downward-sloping resistance trend line is more powerful than a break below its support trend line. Similarly, a rising wedge is thought of as a bearish pattern.

Ideally, volume dries up when the security is in the wedge, and then the breakout occurs on heavy volume.

Figure 3.4

A wedge pattern in iShares FTSE/Xinhua China 25 (FXI). | Courtesy AIQ

A wedge pattern is displayed in Figure 3.4. In this chart for iShares FTSE/Xinhua China 25 (FXI), the wedge is downward-sloping, so this is a bullish pattern. The bullish wedge pattern is even more powerful because the pattern developed while the ETF was in an overall uptrend. Since this is a downward-sloping wedge, the buy signal occurs when the top resistance trend line is broken.

FINAL THOUGHTS

We can get caught up in the details of crazy names and formations of chart patterns, but you will see that nearly every pattern has one thing in common: sideways movement. Rather than entering a security when it is in a steep up or downtrend, chartists prefer to enter after some sideways movement.

For a security in an uptrend, buy after a short period of sideways movement. It is like a sprinter in a track-and-field meet—he runs very fast, but needs to stop and rest so that he can sprint again. Of course, the same holds true for securities in a downtrend.

The length of a chart is significant. A completed pattern on a weekly chart implies a long-term move, while a pattern on a real-time chart may forecast a move that will last only part of the trading day.

It is also important to look at higher time frames. When evaluating a pattern on a daily chart, use a weekly chart to determine the longer-term trend. Along the same line, when evaluating a pattern on a weekly chart, use a monthly chart to determine the longer-term trend. The break in a pattern will most often be in the direction of the trend in the higher time frame chart.

Identifying chart patterns works well for individual stocks because it shows areas where buyers and sellers typically emerge. The same holds true for ETFs, but with ETFs, the tops and bottoms of the pattern signify areas where investors typically buy and sell the underlying stock holdings. For that reason, chartists may choose to perform an additional analysis on the largest stock holdings within an ETF.

Performing pattern analysis is useful, even if you rely on mechanical models to determine portfolio holdings, because it helps identify better entry and exit points. If a trading model says to own iShares Emerging Markets, then we know it is best to buy on a break above a consolidation area. Performing this analysis, as well as Point & Figure analysis from the next chapter, will help improve entry and exit points.

Quick Quiz

1) The length of time that a pattern covers is inconsequential.

   a. True

   b. False

2) A common theme in the chart patterns is:

   a. A period of sideways movement.

   b. Increased volatility over time.

   c. There is no common theme.

3) Which is more important?

   a. a break of a horizontal trend line

   b. a break of a sloping trend line

4) A pattern will eventually be broken to the upside or the downside. What can be used to determine whether prices will likely break to the upside or downside of a pattern?

   a. Seasonality. Some months are better than others for bullish and bearish patterns.

   b. Longer time frames. The trend on a longer-term chart often indicates the direction of the eventual break.

For the answers to this quiz, please visit the Trader's Library Education Corner online at www.TradersLibrary.com/TLEcorner.

4   Point & Figure Charting

Like the traditional bar charts we examined in Chapter 3, point and figure charts graph price activity. This lesser-known form of charting offers some unique advantages over the more traditional bar charts and close-only charts. Specifically, it is easier to identify areas of support and resistance using point and figure charts.

Unlike bar charts, in which the vertical coordinate is based on price and the horizontal coordinate is based on time, the point and figure chart is only concerned with price. Although the years and months are reported on the horizontal axis, they are shown merely to establish a frame of reference. Because time is not a factor, small fluctuations in price are often not charted. Without these disturbances, support and resistance areas become clear, and it is easier to locate chart patterns.

> *Because point and figure charts are concerned only with price, support and resistance levels are more easily identified on them.*

Xs AND Os

I like to think of this charting method as "John Madden charting" because it deals with Xs and Os. Vertical columns of Xs represent increasing prices, and Os signify decreasing prices. Each X or O represents a specific increment of change in price, which is called the box size.

For example, each X may represent a $2 increase in the price of the stock. Every time the stock increases by $2, an X is plotted. Time is irrelevant, so it does not matter how long it takes for the security to make the $2 advance.

When Xs are being plotted, the security is advancing. Typically, the security must fall by three times the box size before a new column of Os will appear to indicate a trend reversal. In our example of a $2 box size, a stock must fall by $6 (three times $2) before a new column of Os is plotted. The three-box reversal is what eliminates all minor and sometimes confusing fluctuations.

Here is the good news: you do not have to know how to plot point and figure charts to use them. Their interpretation is easy, and several web-based charting services, such as StockCharts.com, plot this style of charts for free.

SUPPORT AND RESISTANCE

> **Support**: A price level where buying often takes place.
>
> **Resistance**: A price level where selling often takes place.

There are advantages and disadvantages to all charting methods. One advantage to using point and figure charts is that they make it easier to identify important support and resistance levels because the Xs and Os tend to end at the same level.

Figure 4.1 shows how easily you can identify support and resistance using point and figure charting. Early in the Utilities SPDR (XLU) chart, support is found near $37, an area where three columns of Os end at the same level (upper trend line). Support was broken on the fourth test, when the chart turned bearish. As is sometimes the case, the stock then rallied back to its previous support level and sellers once again emerged. In October, the ETF saw heavy selling, as seen by the long column of Os.

For resistance levels, look for a level where several columns of Xs end at the same level. Beginning in October, XLU began to move sideways.

Figure 4.1

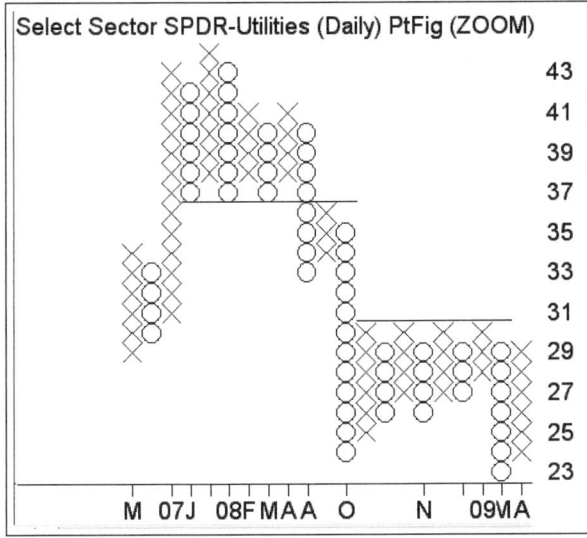

The upper trend line shows an area of support. The lower trend line shows an area of resistance.

Courtesy AIQ

Figure 4.2

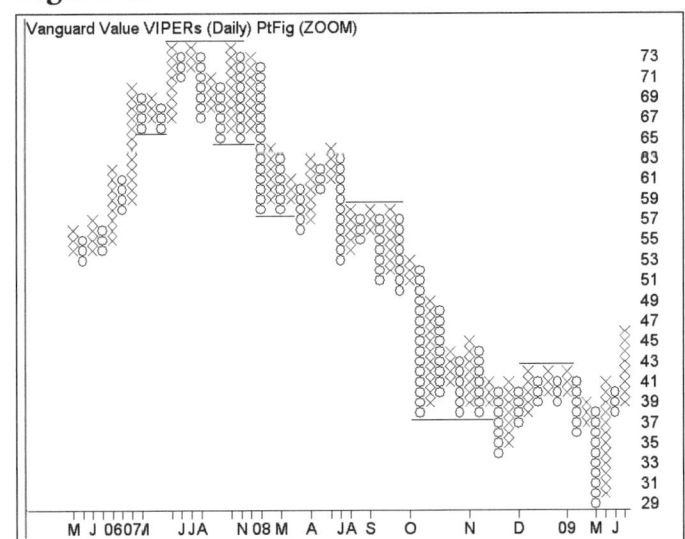

Trend lines show areas of support or resistance.

Courtesy AIQ

Point & Figure Charting

Notice the $31 resistance level where four columns of Xs end (lower trend line). That is resistance. This chart turns bullish, and the security can be purchased once this resistance is penetrated.

Figure 4.2, showing Vanguard Value (VTV), provides another demonstration of how easy it is to identify support and resistance using point and figure charts. Once again, look for areas where Xs or Os end at the same level. We have placed trend lines on the chart to help identify these areas.

POINT & FIGURE CHART PATTERNS

In point and figure charting, a buy signal is registered on a chart when one column of Xs moves higher than the previous column of Xs. The theory behind a buy signal is that the security is able to rise above a level where sellers previously appeared and drove prices lower. The security then remains on a buy until a column of Os falls below a previous column of Os.

Important moves follow periods of sideways movement.

Using this methodology, a lot of buy and sell signals occur. Which signals are best? Patterns can be identified that point toward the more significant buy and sell signals. Fortunately, they are mostly the same patterns that were featured in Chapter 3, and they follow the same theory that important moves follow periods of sideways movement.

Triple-Top Buy and Triple-Bottom Sell

Although the name is different, the triple-top buy and triple-bottom sell pattern is similar to the rectangle pattern from Chapter 3. The triple-top buy is a bullish pattern in which two rally attempts fail at the same level (i.e., two columns of Xs end at or near the same level), but on the next attempt, the security rises above the resistance level.

The triple-bottom sell is just the opposite—the security falls, but finds support at the same area, and on the next attempt, it falls below the previous lows, registering its sell signal.

Figure 4.3, WisdomTree LargeCap Dividend Fund (DLN), shows two examples of triple-bottom sell patterns. At the start of 2008, DLN fell to the same level on two occasions (two columns of Os end at the same level), and each time, buyers emerged. On the third decline, however, support was broken. The triple-bottom sell signal is complete.

Figure 4.3

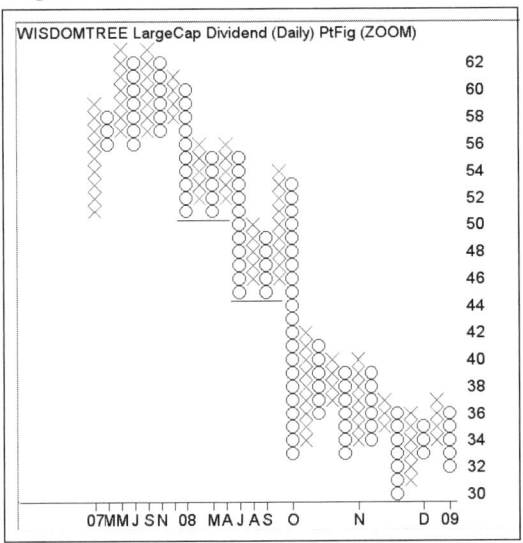

Two triple-bottom sell signals. | Courtesy AIQ

By summer, DLN began moving sideways again. It fell to the same level, and support broke on the third column of Os, thereby registering another triple-bottom sell (lower trend line). Remember my sprinter analogy from Chapter 3—where the sprinter runs, rests, and then runs again? That is what happened here.

In this example, there were two tests of a level and then a breakout. The pattern also holds true if there are three or more tests before the breakout. In fact, the more a level is tested, the more powerful the eventual breakout will be.

Figure 4.4 shows two triple-top patterns (the trend lines mark the top of each pattern), but the second one is preferred. That is because selling became less intense as the pattern developed. During the pattern, each column of Os ended at a higher level than the previous column of Os. We have drawn an upward-sloping trend line to highlight this attractive formation.

Figure 4.4

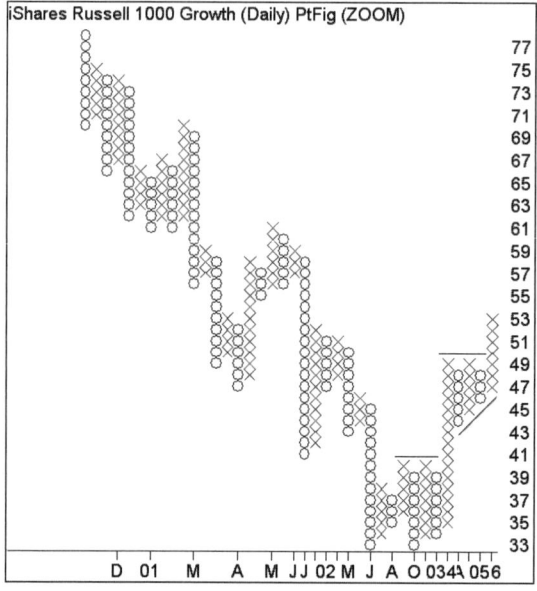

Two triple-top buy signals. There are rising bottoms on the second pattern, making it more attractive.

| Courtesy AIQ

> **Go Further**
>
> There is a triple-bottom pattern near the start of the chart. Can you find it?

Spread Triple-Top Buy and Spread Triple-Bottom Sell

The spread triple-top or triple-bottom is a very broad formation and can take a lot of time to develop. The buy signal is generated when the security penetrates three level tops. The opposite is true for the spread triple-bottom. An example of a spread triple-bottom is found in Figure 4.5. The sell signal is registered when the level bottom of Os is penetrated (see the trend line break). During the time of the spread triple-bottom, other patterns may have occurred. In fact, we see that a triple-bottom sell signal was registered late in the pattern (see shorter trend line).

Figure 4.5

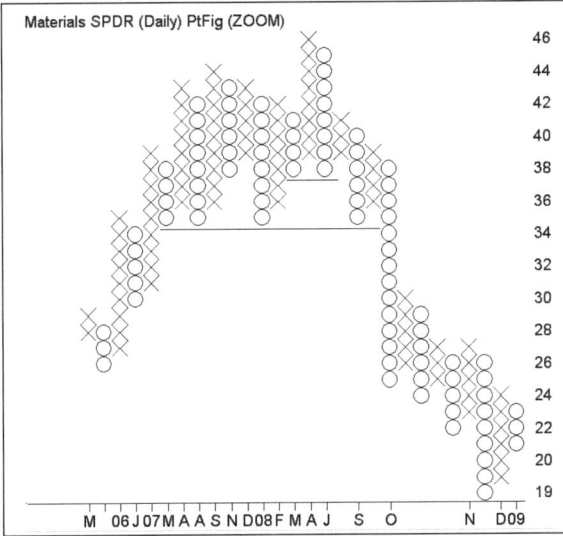

Spread triple-bottom pattern. | Courtesy AIQ

Bullish and Bearish Catapult

The bullish catapult formation starts with a triple-top pattern. Instead of moving straight up after a triple-top buy signal, however, the security has enough of a correction to form a column of Os. The correction is short, and the security reverses to the upside from a higher level than its previous correction. The reverse is true for a bearish catapult.

Figure 4.6 shows a bullish catapult. A triple-top buy signal was registered at $46. It rallied a little after that signal but then reversed and retested the breakout. Finally, it moved higher once again and made a final column of Xs that was higher than the previous column of Xs.

Symmetrical Triangle

You may need a trained eye to find a symmetrical triangle pattern on a bar chart. Finding one in a point and figure chart, however, is easier. This pattern requires at least five columns, and there is a series of higher bottoms and lower tops. For a bullish pattern, the buy comes when the security rises

Figure 4.6

Bullish catapult pattern.

Courtesy AIQ

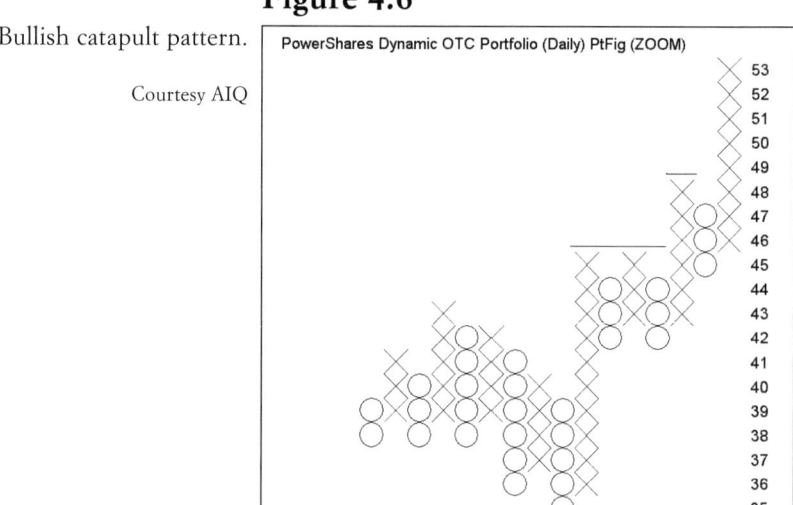

Figure 4.7

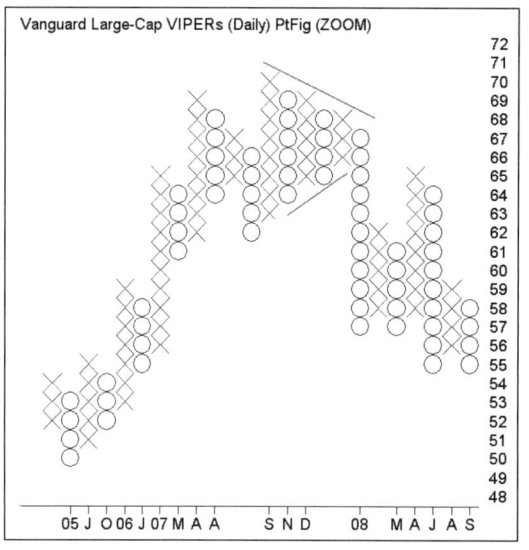

Symmetrical triangle pattern.

Courtesy AIQ

and moves above the previous column of Xs. The opposite is true for the bearish pattern.

Figure 4.7 shows a symmetrical triangle in the Vanguard Large-Cap VIPERS. We have placed trend lines on the pattern to help identify the formation. During the pattern, the rallies are weaker than the previous rallies (lower columns of Xs) and each drop was less than the previous drop (increasing columns of Os). In this case, the break came to the downside. A sell is registered at about $64 when the lower trend line is broken and the column of Os moves below the previous column of Os. This is the least common of the point and figure patterns.

PUTTING IT ALL TOGETHER

As you view point and figure charts, you will quickly identify the patterns covered in this chapter. Practice makes perfect, so scanning through charts and identifying patterns is a useful exercise. You will find that almost every ETF will contain at least one of the patterns we have discussed. In Figure 4.8, there are several patterns. At point A, a triple-bottom sell is registered, point B shows a bearish catapult pattern, and point C shows a triple-top buy signal. Once you have learned to spot them historically, you will better be able to identify the patterns as they develop.

Again, however, we can fall into the trap of looking for specific patterns when the general concepts matter most. The biggest moves come after periods of sideways movement. Higher volatility comes after periods of lower volatility. In all of our patterns, sideways movement happens before trades are placed.

Point and figure charting was not designed to eliminate bar charts. Each charting method has its advantages. With point and figure charting, you can more easily identify important chart patterns, as well as support and resistance levels.

Figure 4.8

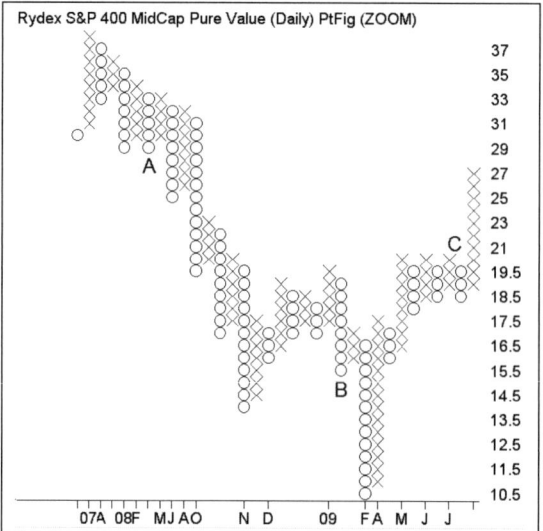

This chart shows triple-bottom (A), bullish catapult (B), and triple-top patterns (C). | Courtesy AIQ

Quick Quiz

1) In point and figure charting, Xs represent increasing prices and Os represent decreasing prices.

   a. True

   b. False

2) A triple top is a bearish pattern.

   a. True

   b. False

3) When it comes to point and figure charting, the _____ is inconsequential.

   a. X axis

   b. Y axis

For the answers to this quiz, please visit the Trader's Library Education Corner online at www.TradersLibrary.com/TLEcorner.

5 Technical Indicators and ETF Volume

The usefulness of technical indicators is a controversial subject. Many books tout their effectiveness, but others point to some exotic, far-fetched indicators and treat them with great skepticism. In some ways, both views are right. Still, if you are going to analyze an ETF, it is worth looking at technical indicators.

WHICH INDICATORS SHOULD YOU USE?

Technical indicators use mathematical formulas based on a security's price and volume data. Many successful traders do not use technical indicators; they simply look at price action because that is what represents supply and demand. Other successful traders use a couple of indicators because these indicators give information that is not readily seen in a chart. Very few, if any, successful traders use a lot of indicators in their everyday trading. Doing so is not necessary. When an analysis software package highlights how it has "hundreds of technical indicators," that is simply the work of the marketing department. If you decide to use technical indicators in your process, pick two or three that fit your style, learn their behavior well, and ignore the hundreds of other indicators.

Finding the "crystal ball" indicator is a never-ending journey. In a sense, technical indicators have a lot in common with diets; new diets appear all the time—some more popular than others—but each one fades away as people move on to the next "new and improved" diet plan. It is the same thing with indicators. People often focus too much on the search for the perfect indicator.

Which indicators should you use? That is a personal decision. Indicators that work well for one person may not work well for others. Yes, it requires work, but successful traders have undergone the tedious process of researching the many technical indicators and choosing the ones that fit their trading style.

PRICE-BASED INDICATORS AND THE SECURITY TREND

The majority of technical indicators are calculated from the price action of the underlying security. Some of these indicators work well in trending markets while others are best in consolidating or sideways markets. Therefore, it is important to determine the trend of the security before analyzing it with an indicator.

In Table 5.1, we have classified some well-known indicators into two categories—those that work well in trending environments, and those that work well in non-trending environments.

Generally, indicators that work well in non-trending market environments are those that give overbought/oversold readings. The theory is that when a security rises too far too fast, it becomes overbought and therefore retreats. The opposite is true for oversold conditions.

These indicators work well in non-trending environments because an overbought reading is registered whenever the security rallies to the upper end of its trading range. Conversely, the security becomes oversold when it nears the lower end of its trading range.

Indicators that work well in trending environments are generally those that tend to remain positive as long as the security continues to rise, or those that remain negative as long as the security falls. A common element in many of these indicators is the use of moving averages.

Table 5.1: Indicator Classification	
Trending	**Non-trending**
AD Oscillator	RSI
Directional Movement Index (DMI)	Stochastic
MACD	
Moving Averages	
SK-SD	

Non-trending Indicators

To determine the effectiveness of a non-trending indicator, we will look at the SPDR S&P 500 (SPY) during a non-trending market environment. Figure 5.1 shows the SPY with its RSI indicator—an indicator that works well for non-trending securities. An RSI buy signal is registered when the indicator moves out of oversold territory by rising above the lower horizontal line (corresponding to a value of 30). A sell is registered when the indicator falls below the upper horizontal line (corresponding to a value of 70).

Notice that as the SPY nears the top of the trading range, the RSI moves above 70, indicating an overbought reading. Shortly after reaching overbought, the market falls and the RSI registers its sell signal. Conversely, when the S&P 500 falls to the bottom of the range, the RSI reaches oversold and a low is near. In a non-trending market, the RSI indicator works very well.

However, the RSI indicator loses its effectiveness when a strong trend develops. In Figure 5.2, we see the SPY in late 2006, during a strong uptrend. During the entire advance, the indicator never gave a buy signal, but registered many sell signals (see the down arrows) even as the market moved higher. The RSI, as well as the other non-trending indicators, will almost always have you exit from strong trending markets too early.

Figure 5.1

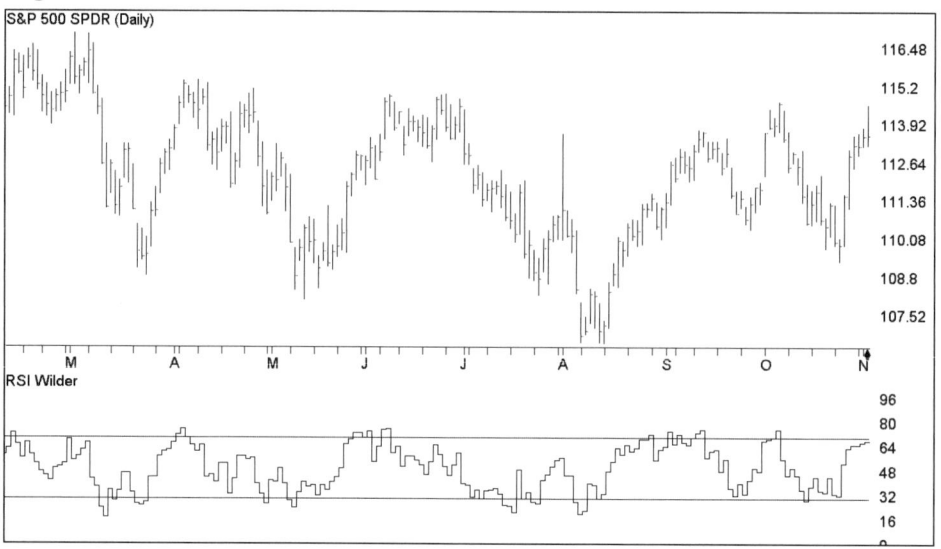

The RSI indicator works well for SPY, a non-trending security. | Courtesy AIQ

Figure 5.2

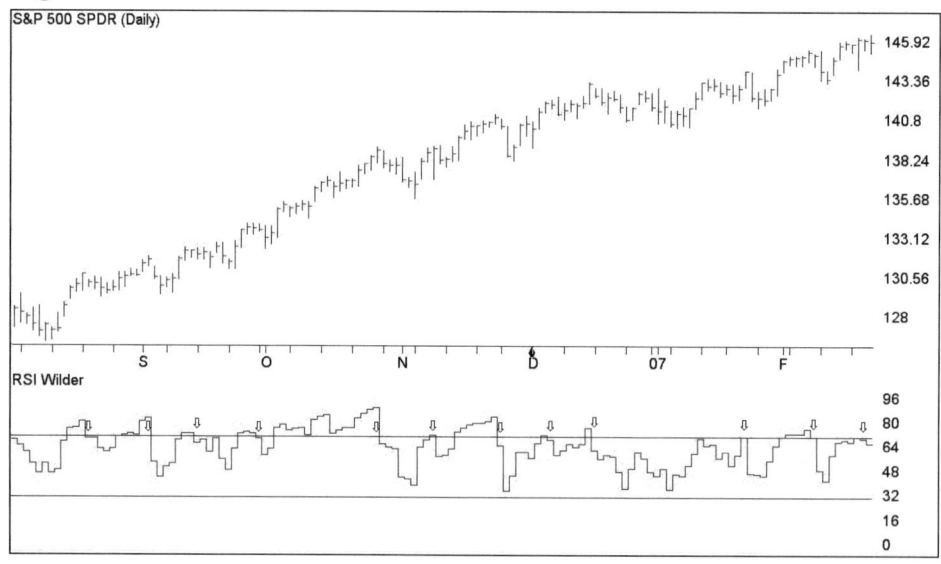

The RSI indicator, using its standard interpretation, loses effectiveness for this trending security. | Courtesy AIQ

Trending Indicators

Now we will examine the effectiveness of an indicator that works well in a trending market environment. Figure 5.3 displays an uptrending SPY along with its Directional Movement Index (DMI, or DirMov in Figure 5.3). Using the DMI, a buy is registered when the indicator moves above zero and a sell is registered when it falls below zero. In the uptrending S&P 500 chart, the DMI remained positive for the majority of the market advance.

The DMI works well for the uptrending market, but it loses its effectiveness in non-trending environments. Most of the trades turn out to be whipsaws, and the trades come in the middle of the range rather than the upper and lower ends of the range.

Modifying Indicator Readings

We have seen in our analysis that when an indicator that works well in a non-trending market is applied to a trending security, it gives bad signals against the trend. Does this mean the indicator should be ignored? Not necessarily. By making adjustments to an indicator's interpretation, we can effectively apply a non-trending indicator to a trending market.

Figure 5.3

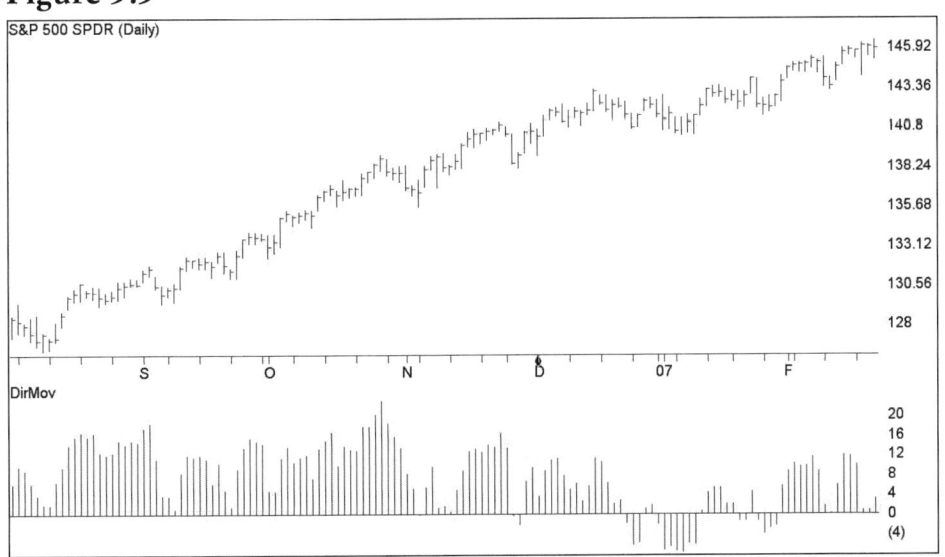

The Directional Movement Index works well for this trending security. | Courtesy AIQ

Technical Indicators and ETF Volume

The first adjustment is to simply ignore all signals against the trend of the security. We have seen these indicators give frequent sell signals during a strong advance, but these signals should be ignored. This does not mean you should not have an exit system in place; it simply means that the exit system should not involve the use of non-trending indicators.

The second adjustment is to change the requirements for buy and sell signals so that the indicator gives more signals in the direction of the overall trend. The Stochastic, or RSI, will rarely give buy signals in an uptrending market. As a result, the "oversold" levels should be adjusted upward so the indictor will give buy signals. For these two indicators, a level below 50 may represent an oversold buy point. Applying this method to the SPY in Figure 5.2, overbought sell signals are ignored because the market is trending up. Using 50 as an oversold level, most of the minor pullbacks in the market result in an RSI buy signal. When using a non-trending indicator in a trending market, be sure to only use the signals in the direction of the overall trend.

Conclusion

Many indicators can be classified into two categories: those that work in trending markets, and those that work in non-trending markets. Unless adjustments are made to an indicator's interpretation, you can get into trouble if you use the wrong type of indicator in a given market environment. Those who like to trade in sideways markets, buying low and selling high for frequent but small profits, should use non-trending indicators. Growth investors who buy into uptrends should either use trend-following indicators or a modified version of a non-trending indicator.

PRICE AND VOLUME-BASED INDICATORS

Most technical indicators are based solely on price. Price is the most important component in technical analysis, but volume is important as well. Volume is thought of as the fuel that sustains a trend. What happens to a security on high-volume days is more important than what happens on low-volume days. For this reason, several technical indicators are based on both price and volume.

This poses a problem for ETF traders. Just because there is a volume spike in the ETF does not mean there were volume spikes in the stocks that the ETF holds. An equity ETF tracks a market index, so it is possible for an ETF to fall in value at the same time that there are more buy orders than sell orders. Remember, ETFs are open-end funds, so more shares are created when there is a large institutional buy order. This differs from stocks. If a large buyer enters a stock, he will drive the stock higher. Whereas the total number of shares of an equity are generally fixed, the total number of shares in an ETF often change weekly.

> *An ETF's movement is not determined by buyers and sellers. Instead, its movement depends on the action of its underlying index.*

This is easier explained with an actual example. In Figure 5.4, we see a spike in volume on December 31 shown by the arrow on the volume chart. On that day, the iShares Regional Banks ETF (IAT) closed on its daily high point and volume was six times its average. Apparently a large money player, or perhaps multiple players, wanted to own this ETF at the end of the year.

This iShares Regional Banks ETF (IAT) tracks an index of banking stocks, and those stocks did not have a similar spike in volume. Figure 5.5 shows the same ETF, but this time its volume is created by summing the volume of its ten largest stock holdings. Notice that on December 31 (the down arrow in the chart), there was no spike in volume. The securities that the ETF tracks show that there was not a mad rush to enter banking stocks. The volume on the Regional Banks ETF was giving a misleading picture of what was happening to the securities that determine the ETF's movement.

There are plenty of other differences in volume readings between these two charts. Notice only one of the two January volume spikes in Figure 5.4 appears in the calculated volume chart in Figure 5.5. Also, the ETF shows below-average volume in late January, whereas Figure 5.5 shows continued high volume during the same period.

Figure 5.4

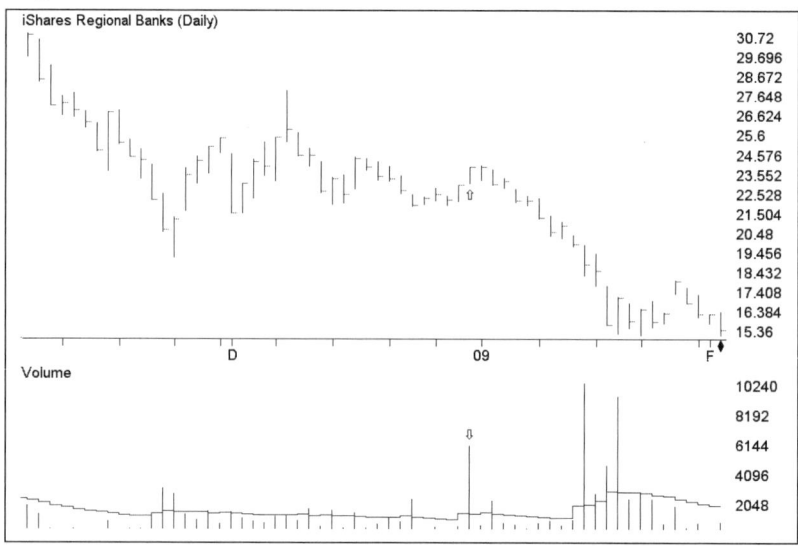

iShares Regional Banks with the ETF's volume. | Courtesy AIQ

Figure 5.5

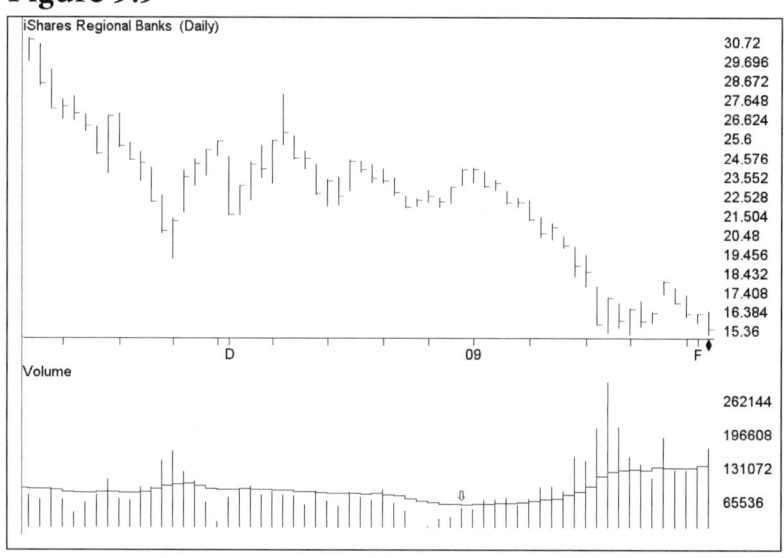

iShares Regional Banks with volume calculated using the ETF's volume.
| Courtesy AIQ

Another example using the same fund is found on November 5, 2010. On that day, the majority of bank stocks had high volume. In Figure 5.6, we see volume spikes in all of the iShares Regional Bank's top four holdings. For anyone analyzing volume or using technical indicators that are based on volume, this was an important day.

Yet, those that limited their analysis to the ETF's volume failed to see the volume spikes. Figure 5.7 shows the fund along with its trading volume. The volume on November 5 does not stand out—it was just average. The fund's trading volume does not reflect the activity of the fund's holdings. Remember, it is the movement of these holdings that drives the fund's price higher and lower.

Most technicians who have analyzed price and volume on stocks are applying the same techniques to ETFs. They assume what works for one also works for another. Unfortunately, when it comes to volume, that is not the case—it is like thinking that a bicycle built for speed on the road must also work well on dirt trails. Not so.

> *If you are going to analyze volume, then it is best to look at the volume of the stocks that an ETF holds rather than looking at the volume of the ETF itself. This is especially true for low-volume ETFs.*

Let's see how this can affect a technical indicator. One of the most popular volume indicators is On-Balance Volume (OBV), developed by Joseph Granville. Figure 5.8 shows iShares Networking (IGN) along with its Volume and OBV indicator. The periodic huge volume spikes show that there will be a problem in volume-based indicators. Notice the spiky movement in OBV on those days, featured in Figure 5.8.

Compare that OBV to the indicator in Figure 5.9, where volume is once again calculated by summing the volume of the ETF's ten largest stock holdings. Here, volume is more consistent and the OBV indicator is a better reflection of what is actually happening to the ETF's holdings.

Figure 5.6

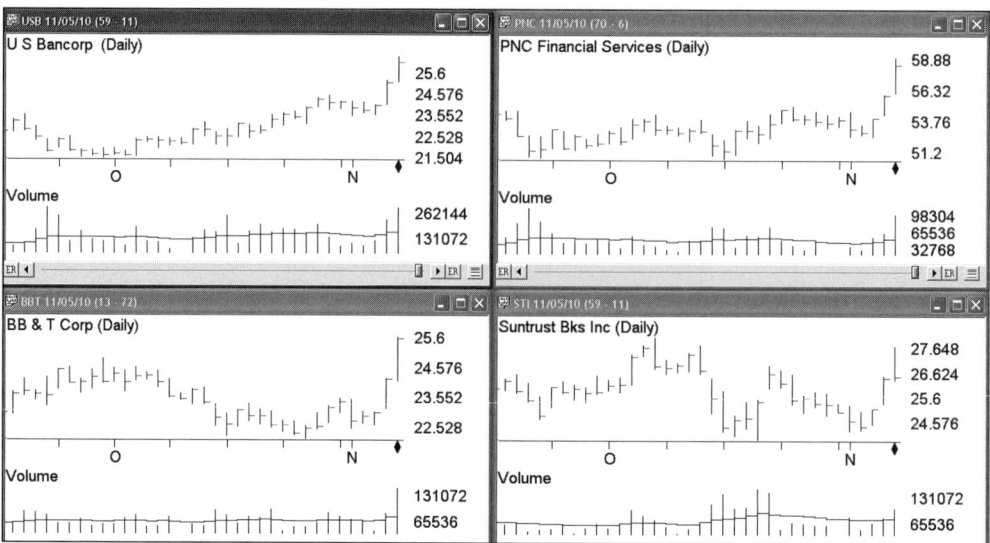

Volume spike in iShares Regional Bank's top holdings. | Courtesy AIQ

Figure 5.7

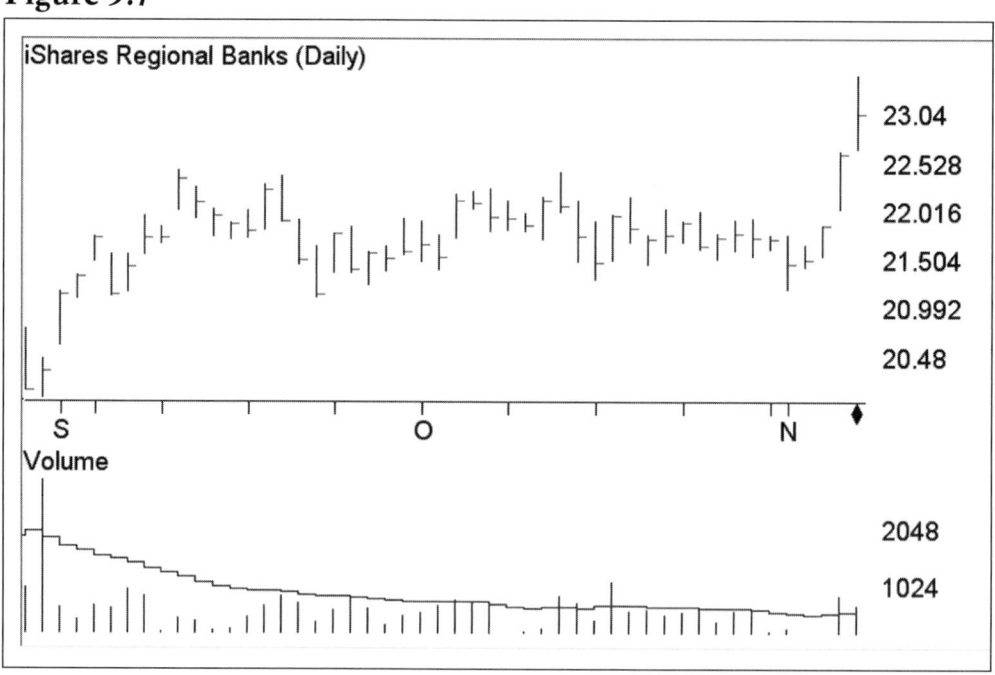

iShares Regional Banks with trading volume. | Courtesy AIQ

Figure 5.8

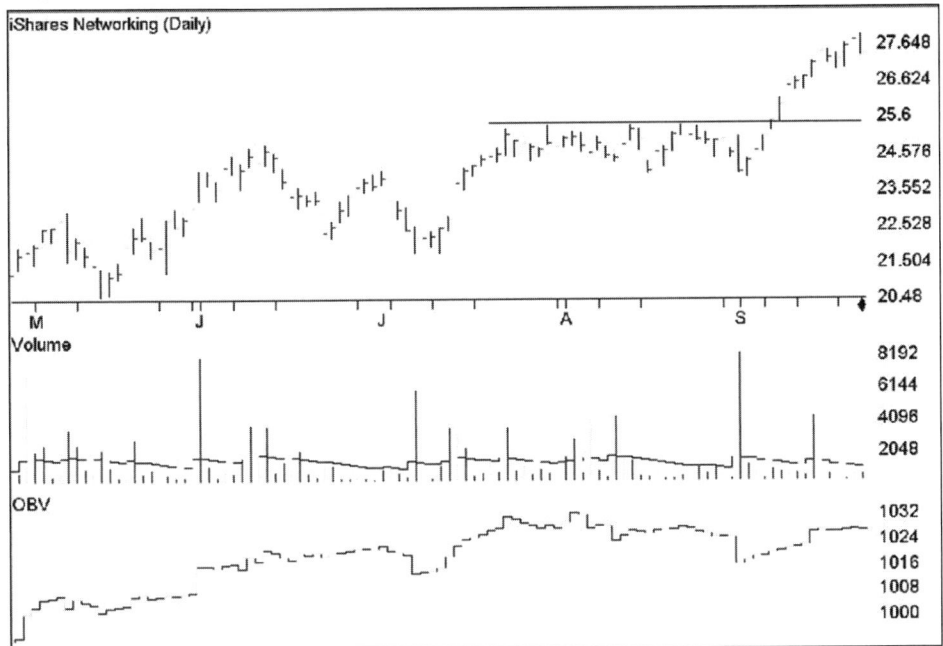

iShares Networking with volume and OBV indicator. | Courtesy AIQ

Figure 5.9

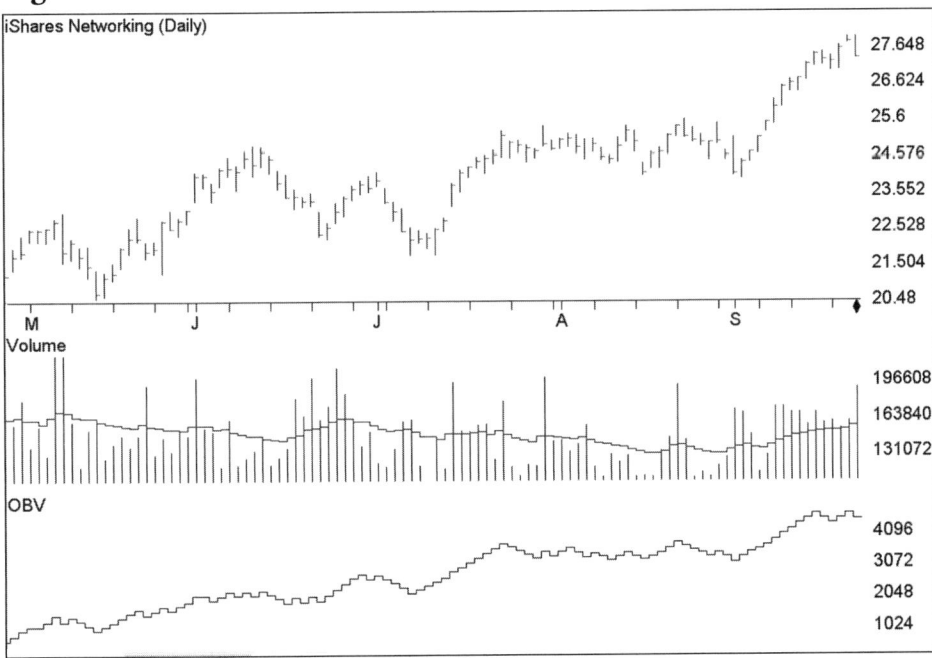

iShares Networking along with its volume and OBV calculated by summing the volume from the ETF's ten largest stock holdings. | Courtesy AIQ

Technical Indicators and ETF Volume

This makes a difference. OBV using the ETF's volume statistics hit a new one-month low in early July, whereas OBV calculated on the stocks did not. OBV using the ETF's volume statistics peaked in August, whereas OBV calculated on the stocks was hitting new highs throughout most of September.

This discrepancy is reduced on high-volume ETFs, but we clearly see that running indicators utilizing an ETF's volume is a case of garbage in, garbage out. When analyzing an ETF's volume, use a summation of the volume on the ETF's largest stock holdings.

Analyzing Volume

The key to analyzing price and volume is this: what happens to the price is more important on days of heavy volume compared to days of light volume. Think about the game show *Who Wants to Be a Millionaire*. When a contestant is stumped by a question, he or she has an opportunity to poll the audience for the answer. If the audience votes overwhelmingly for one answer, then it is very likely that that answer is correct. This equates to a day where the price advances and closes near its daily high price on high volume.

> *What happens to price is more important on days of heavy volume compared to days of light volume.*

If, however, few people in the audience vote and there is no consensus about the answer, then this equates to a day where there is little movement in the security and volume is light.

Ideally, a stock or ETF rises with above-average volume and closes near the high of the day. This implies that big-money players want into the security and that it is under accumulation. It would be bearish, however, for the security to close near the low point of the day with above-average volume. That would imply that big-money players do not want to hold the security overnight.

Analyst Marc Chaikin took this concept and created a set of indicators that rewards securities that close near their daily high on above-average volume. His Volume Accumulation Percent (VApct) indicator, also called the Money Flow Oscillator, combines volume readings with the relationship between the closing price and the day's price range. A second indicator, Money Flow, is a running total of an accumulation factor (see the formula later in this chapter).

Money Flow Indicator

Money Flow is my favorite price and volume indicator because it measures whether the security is being accumulated or distributed by big-money players. The indicator turns strong when the security closes near its daily high with above-average volume (a sign of accumulation). The indicator falls when the security closes near its daily low with above-average volume (a sign of distribution). There is little movement in the indicator if the security closes in the middle of its daily range, or if volume was light.

> **Divergence** is the comparison of the security's price to technical indicators. A divergence occurs when the indicator is moving in the opposite direction from the price of the security.

Unlike most indicators, Money Flow can fall when the security is rising and rise when a security is falling. Money Flow will fall anytime a security rises in value but closes in the lower half of the day's range, indicating that investors are unloading shares at the higher prices.

Money Flow works best as an indicator for growth investing. When you buy an uptrending ETF, you can use Money Flow to confirm the security's strength. Ideally, you want to own an ETF that is in a steady and consistent uptrend. At the same time, you want its Money Flow indicator to also be in a steady and consistent uptrend. If Money Flow is consistently strong, then its sister indicator, VApct, will generally remain above zero.

A good example is iShares Realty Majors (ICF) in Figure 5.10, along with indicators calculated from the volume statistics of the ETF's largest stock

Figure 5.10

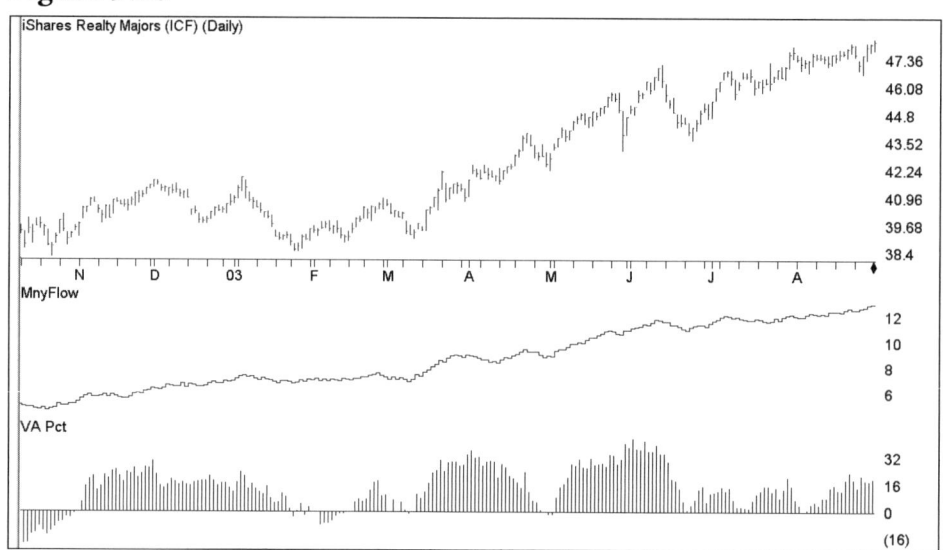

iShares Realty Majors with very strong Money Flow and VApct. | Courtesy AIQ

holdings. The first indication that a strong advance was approaching came in January when Realty Majors hit a new low but Money Flow was in a slight uptrend. Growth investors, however, would not be interested until April when this ETF began hitting new highs. As the ETF stair-stepped higher, Money Flow confirmed the move by also hitting new highs. In fact, Realty Major's Money Flow was stronger than the ETF. After the late April and June pullbacks, Money Flow hit a new high before the ETF did. In August, when the ETF was drifting sideways, Money Flow continued to hit new highs. That is ideal.

Remember, Money Flow should not be calculated on the ETF's volume. Instead, a summation of the volume of the ETF's largest holdings should be used in the Money Flow calculation.

Money Flow and VApct are the same indicator, they are just charted differently. Because Money Flow was strong, its VApct remained above zero most of the time. I find divergences are more easily seen using a Money Flow chart, while strength over time is more easily identified using a VApct chart.

PUTTING IT ALL TOGETHER

Growth Investing

Growth investors like to buy high and sell higher. Just like surfers, they wait for a big wave and then ride that wave until it weakens. Let's apply the techniques we have highlighted from this chapter along with those from the chart pattern chapters to form a growth-investing entry system.

In our chart pattern chapters, we saw that an attractive setup occurs when an uptrending security undergoes a period of sideways movement or consolidation. As the ETF drifts sideways, it is ideal if its Money Flow indicator continues its move higher. An example is found in Figure 5.11. Consumer Goods (IYK) moved higher from July to September, at which time it began to drift sideways for about a month. While the ETF was drifting sideways in September and October, its Money Flow continued its uptrend and was hitting new highs. This implied that the underlying stocks were under accumulation and that Consumer Goods would break above its consolidation.

Figure 5.11

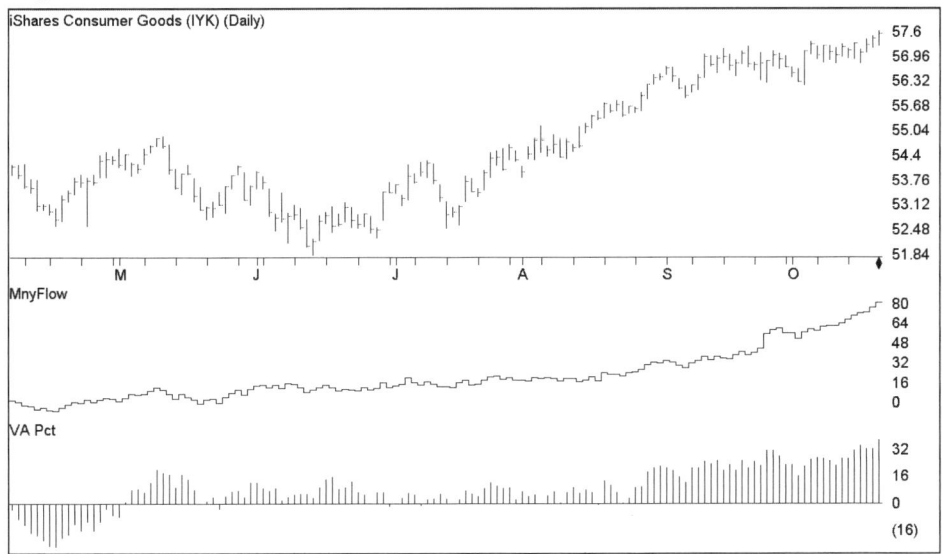

iShares Consumer Goods drifted in September and October, but its Money Flow remained strong. | Courtesy AIQ

Notice also that the strength in Money Flow began in May, well before the ETF. This is more easily seen in the VApct, as it remained above zero for all but a few days in May through October. It works to buy uptrending securities that have recently paused, especially if Money Flow rises during the pause. This is true for both ETFs and stocks.

> *Buy uptrending securities that have recently paused, especially if Money Flow rises during the pause.*

Bottom Fishing

Identifying major lows is difficult. Instead of trying to pick the exact low, it is often best to let the security establish the low before entry. Still, bottom fishers want to get into a move early. A tool that I find helpful in identifying possible tops or bottoms is to look for divergences using a momentum indicator on a weekly chart. An example is found in Figure 5.12. Most any momentum indicator will work, but the indicator on this chart represents the difference between a three- and ten-week simple moving average. Notice during the March low, Consumer Discretionary SPDR (XLY) remained

Figure 5.12

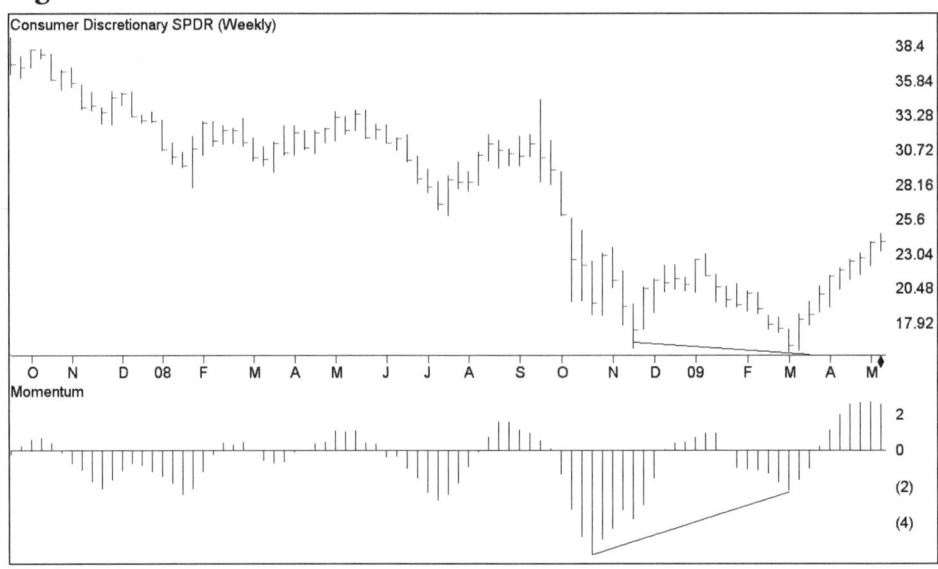

Consumer Discretionary SPDR has a positive divergence in its momentum indicator.
Courtesy AIQ

in a pattern of lower lows. Momentum, however, had a large positive divergence when it made a higher low. By May, momentum was higher than any time in the past several years.

The daily charts on weak stocks always look bad because the stocks are trending lower and often underperforming. Although Money Flow and VApct are not great bottom-fishing indicators, it is nice to see an improvement in their readings. I like to see VApct above zero.

Quantifying the Analysis

If I told you to jump off a bridge, would you do it? Of course not. That is why I will attempt to quantify most of what is written in this book. When it comes to testing entry rules, the most effective system I have found does not even involve a technical indicator. It simply looks for an uptrending stock that has paused for ten days. Remember, the theme of our charting chapters was to buy stocks after a period of consolidation. Just as a sprinter needs to rest periodically, bullish securities also need to pause before making another run.

Specifically, the rule states that the security needs to have increased by at least 50 percent in the past 66 business days (i.e., approximately three months), but its highest value in the past ten days needs to have occurred ten days ago (that is the pausing requirement in our system). So the security is moving higher, at least 50 percent in three months, but it has temporarily paused. This simple system produces incredibly high returns.

To run a larger and longer backtest, we can test the system on stocks. A ten-year backtest is found in Figure 5.13. The 1,500 stocks in the S&P 1500 were examined using a fixed holding period of 60 business days (87 calendar days, or approximately three months). During this ten-year period, there were 1,985 trades with an average gain per trade of 9.71 percent. If you bought the S&P 500 instead, the average trade would have been 0.91 percent.

Can a Money Flow indicator add value? If you add a requirement that states the stocks must also have a VApct indicator above the 30 level, then the average trade jumps to 10.85 percent with 234 trades.

Figure 5.13

```
Growth
                                              Winners         Losers         Neutral
                                           ==========     ==========     ==========
Number of trades in test:         1985           1181            800               4
Average periods per trade:       87.10          86.86          87.44           87.25

Maximum Profit/Loss:                          353.94 %       (87.42)%
Average Drawdown:              (17.81)%         (9.74)%       (29.82)%
Average Profit/Loss:             9.71 %         29.59 %       (19.60)%
Average SPX Profit/Loss:         0.91 %          3.70 %        (3.22)%

Probability:                                    59.50 %        40.30 %
Average Annual ROI:             40.67 %        124.35 %       (81.82)%
Annual SPX (Buy & Hold):        (1.89)%

Reward/Risk Ratio:               2.23

Start test date:              09/17/99
End test date:                09/17/09

Interval: Daily
Using list: SP1500
Pricing Summary
   Entry price: [Open]
   Exit price: [Open]
Exit Summary
   Hold for 60 periods
```

Testing results from a growth model. | Courtesy AIQ

This confirms that buying stocks that are in strong uptrends but have recently paused is a very effective entry strategy. Requiring a strong VApct indicator slightly increases the effectiveness. But as always, past performance does not guarantee future results.

Running this model on a list of ETFs gives too few trades to be statistically valid, but the point of the analysis is that buying high relative strength securities that have recently paused is an effective entry strategy.

> *Buying high relative strength securities that have recently paused is an effective entry strategy.*

Now let's look to quantify a bottom-fishing entry system. Once again, we will run the model on a list of the S&P 1500 stocks rather than on a list of ETFs.

Doing so will give us more trades and make results more statistically reliable.

For this model, the security must have corrected at least 30 percent sometime between 10 and 50 days ago. Losing 30 percent will give a list of both undervalued stocks and junk stocks that should not be owned. To weed out the junk, we will add the requirement that the security must have a VApct indicator that is above zero, as well as a positive 45-day VApct slope.

The results of a ten-year backtest are found in Figure 5.14. Assuming every trade was acted on, there were 4,812 trades. Using a fixed holding period of 22 business days (approximately one month), the average return per trade was 3.13 percent. If you bought the S&P 500 instead of the stocks, the average return per trade would have been negative 0.50 percent.

Figure 5.14

Citizenkane		Winners	Losers	Neutral
Number of trades in test:	4812	2512	2288	12
Average periods per trade:	32.12	32.03	32.21	32.25
Maximum Profit/Loss:		517.86 %	(85.27)%	
Average Drawdown:	(14.82)%	(6.48)%	(24.06)%	
Average Profit/Loss:	3.13 %	21.85 %	(17.41)%	
Average SPX Profit/Loss:	(0.50)%	2.53 %	(3.83)%	
Probability:		52.20 %	47.55 %	
Average Annual ROI:	35.55 %	249.00 %	(197.35)%	
Annual SPX (Buy & Hold):	(1.89)%			
Reward/Risk Ratio:	1.38			
Start test date:	09/17/99			
End test date:	09/17/09			
Interval: Daily				
Using list: SP1500				
Includes Open Positions (5)				
Pricing Summary				
Entry price: [Open]				
Exit price: [Open]				
Exit Summary				
Hold for 22 periods				

Testing results from a bottom-fishing model. |Courtesy AIQ

These results are impressive considering there were two large bear markets during our testing period. If you bought when stocks fell 30 percent from their highs, then you bought too early in these bear markets.

If you ran this screening on a list of the iShares sector ETFs using volume calculated from the stock holdings, then there were 593 trades with an average gain per trade of 1.6 percent. Past performance does not guarantee future results, but the test still holds its value.

It is easy to back-fit a model to make it work. That is not the case here. I wrote about the growth model in a December 2000 technical publication and wrote about the bottom-fishing model in an April 2000 publication.

> **Email the Author**
> If you would like to read these publications, send me an email at dvomund@etfportfolios.net

Money Flow and Volume Accumulation Percent Formula Calculation

Accumulation/Distribution Factor Calculation:

$$(((close - low) - (high - close)) / (high - low)) \times volume$$

Keeping a running total of this formula creates the Money Flow indicator. Volume Accumulation Percent, or Money Flow Oscillator, is the 21-day sum of the above formula divided by the 21-day sum of the day's volume.

Quick Quiz

1) What has the greatest influence on the price movement of an ETF?

   a. The ETF holdings

   b. Buyers and sellers

2) Can an ETF rise in value at the same time that there are more sell orders than buy orders?

   a. Yes

   b. No

3) What is the most bullish scenario for a security?

   a. The security closes near its daily high with above average volume.

   b. The security closes near its daily high with below average volume.

   c. The security closes near its daily low with above average volume.

   d. The security closes near its daily low with below average volume.

For the answers to this quiz, please visit the Trader's Library Education Corner online at www.TradersLibrary.com/TLEcorner.

6 Market Timing

After the 2007 to 2009 bear market, people began declaring that buy-and-hold was dead and that timing the market was essential. I am not in that camp. I am still of the opinion that over the long run, the market goes higher. What has changed is the definition of "the long run."

For the ten years from 1999 to 2009, the S&P 500 was essentially flat. A lost decade has happened on two previous occasions dating back to the 1920s; so it is rare, but not unprecedented. Still, over long periods, the market's trend is higher.

From 1928 through 2008, stocks returned an average of around nine percent. That return holds steady during periods of 25 years or more. The market does not move in a straight line, however. Over the past 80 years, there were only seven years when the market's gain came within three percent of its historical average!

Timing the market (i.e., being in when the market rises and exiting when it falls) is extremely difficult. If the investing public tried to be market timers, I bet they would be worse off. In the past ten years, the market has been flat, but those who time the market without a strong plan tend to buy high and sell low. They have made the period worse than it was. As a money manager, I see how easy it is to get new accounts when the market is high and how hard it is to find clients when the market is low. It is backward.

Timing the market is difficult for professionals, too. Consider how many analysts have gained fame with a good market call only to fall from grace on the market's next move. Few market timers pass the test of time. I find security selection easier than calling overall market moves.

Still, market timing has its place. Anyone who incorporates market timing will reduce the risk and volatility of his or her portfolio. A portfolio that is temporarily in cash is always less volatile than a portfolio that remains fully invested. Market timing reduces portfolio drawdowns, possibly keeping risk-averse investors in the game.

> *Market timing is quite difficult for the investing public and professionals alike; however, incorporating some form of market timing can help to reduce the risk and volatility in a portfolio.*

I do not use a mechanical market-timing model, as I have never found a fully mechanical market-timing system that I am comfortable with. Instead, I use a "weight of the evidence" approach to determine my market outlook. In this chapter, I will discuss some market-timing findings, but for those who want to incorporate market timing into their trading approach, I would recommend subscribing to one of the many market-timing services or investment newsletters.

> **More Info**
> One good resource is Timer Digest (www.timerdigest.com), which is a publication that tracks the market-timing performance of investment newsletters.

Overall, here is a good market timing rule: sell when you want to tell your neighbors how well your portfolio is doing, and buy when you would rather talk about anything other than the market!

The following sections contain some key market timing observations.

THE MARKET IS NON-TRENDING

Moving Average Convergence/Divergence (MACD) Indicator

The Moving Average Convergence/Divergence (MACD) indicator, developed by Gerald Appel, is a price momentum indicator that plots two lines. The first component is the price phase line, which represents the difference between two moving averages. This is the fast line on the indicator. The second component is the signal line, which is a moving average of the price phase line.

How effective is the MACD as a market timing indicator? Our test uses the S&P 500's weekly MACD indicator and registers a buy signal when the price phase line crosses above the signal line and a sell signal when the price phase line crosses below the signal line. When the crossover is to the upside, you go long the S&P 500. That position is closed and moved to the money market when the price phase line crosses below the signal line. Since we are using the indicator in the weekly mode, all trades are known on Friday's close and executed on Monday's opening price.

Figure 6.1

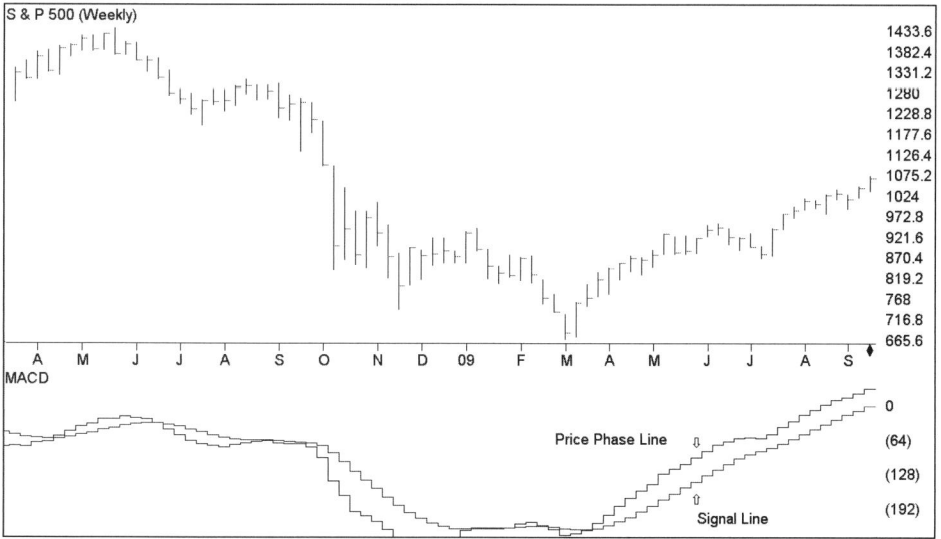

The weekly S&P 500 along with its MACD indicator. This indicator was on a sell for most of the bear market and was on a buy for most of the recovery. | Courtesy AIQ

Market Timing

Figure 6.1 shows how well the indicator can work. Notice the price phase line was below the signal line for most of the 2008 bear market, keeping traders in cash. During the 2009 recovery, the phase line was above the signal line.

The trade-by-trade results of our testing are found in Table 6.1. The section at the left shows times when the weekly MACD indicator is bullish (i.e., the price phase line is above the signal line). Since 1996, trading the S&P 500 during times when the weekly MACD was favorable led to a loss of 15 percent (not annualized). Ouch.

If trading results are poor when buying the S&P 500 during times that the weekly MACD was bullish, then it must be true that trading the S&P 500 when the indicator is bearish would be more profitable.

The section to the right in Table 6.1 shows the results of buying the S&P 500 when the MACD indicator was negative. Amazingly, about 80 percent of the trades were profitable, and the return since 1996, with compounding, was 94 percent.

This does not discredit the MACD indicator. After all, it was designed to be used in a daily format, it is more often applied to stocks, and there are more advanced methods of interpreting the indicator. It is important to know, however, that it is better to go long when the weekly indicator is bearish.

We performed this exercise to demonstrate that the market is typically non-trending. By the time the S&P 500 rises enough to turn the weekly MACD indicator upward, then it is often too late to buy. Only in times when there is a strong trend, such as the period shown in Figure 6.1, does the indicator work well.

I am not suggesting that one should go long on the market when this indicator gives a sell signal. It would be painful to be on the wrong side of the market each time a strong trend develops. Instead, I am demonstrating that by the time the market looks good, it is often ready to turn south, and vice versa.

Table 6.1: S&P 500 Movement for Weekly MACD Crossovers

When MACD is Bullish			When MACD is Bearish		
Buy Date	Sell Date	% Chg	Buy Date	Sell Date	% Chg
12/31/1995	1/12/1996	-2.29	1/12/1996	2/9/1996	9.06
2/9/1996	3/15/1996	-2.27	3/15/1996	5/24/1996	5.78
5/24/1996	6/14/1996	-1.87	6/14/1996	9/20/1996	3.18
9/20/1996	3/21/1997	14.13	3/21/1997	5/16/1997	5.82
5/16/1997	8/29/1997	8.40	8/29/1997	2/6/1998	12.56
2/6/1998	5/22/1998	9.68	5/22/1998	7/17/1998	6.87
7/17/1998	7/24/1998	-3.87	7/24/1998	11/6/1998	0.02
11/6/1998	5/21/1999	16.59	5/21/1999	7/9/1999	5.49
7/9/1999	7/23/1999	-3.30	7/23/1999	11/12/1999	2.89
11/12/1999	1/28/2000	-2.57	1/28/2000	3/24/2000	12.30
3/24/2000	4/14/2000	-11.19	4/14/2000	7/7/2000	9.02
7/7/2000	7/28/2000	-3.99	7/28/2000	8/18/2000	5.06
8/18/2000	9/22/2000	-2.88	9/22/2000	2/2/2001	-6.85
2/2/2001	2/23/2001	-7.68	2/23/2001	4/27/2001	0.58
4/27/2001	8/17/2001	-7.27	8/17/2001	11/2/2001	-6.43
11/2/2001	2/22/2002	0.24	2/22/2002	3/1/2002	3.85
3/1/2002	4/26/2002	-4.90	4/26/2002	10/18/2002	-17.83
10/18/2002	2/7/2003	-6.18	2/7/2003	3/21/2003	7.97
3/21/2003	9/26/2003	11.28	9/26/2003	10/3/2003	3.31
10/3/2003	11/21/2003	0.53	11/21/2003	12/12/2003	3.75
12/12/2003	3/12/2004	4.02	3/12/2004	9/17/2004	1.00
9/17/2004	10/22/2004	-2.91	10/22/2004	10/29/2004	3.14
10/29/2004	1/28/2005	3.64	1/28/2005	2/25/2005	3.41
2/25/2005	3/11/2005	-0.93	3/11/2005	6/10/2005	-0.17
6/10/2005	9/2/2005	1.66	9/2/2005	9/9/2005	1.93
9/9/2005	9/23/2005	-2.11	9/23/2005	11/18/2005	2.71
11/18/2005	4/13/2006	3.27	4/13/2006	4/28/2006	1.67
4/28/2006	5/12/2006	-1.48	5/12/2006	8/18/2006	0.86

| Table 6.1: S&P 500 Movement for Weekly MACD Crossovers ||||||
| When MACD is Bullish ||| When MACD is Bearish |||
Buy Date	Sell Date	% Chg	Buy Date	Sell Date	% Chg
8/18/2006	3/2/2007	6.51	3/2/2007	4/20/2007	7.01
4/20/2007	6/29/2007	1.37	6/29/2007	7/13/2007	3.18
7/13/2007	7/27/2007	-6.03	7/27/2007	10/5/2007	6.69
10/5/2007	11/9/2007	-6.60	11/9/2007	4/11/2008	-8.36
4/11/2008	6/27/2008	-4.06	6/27/2008	8/22/2008	0.97
8/22/2008	9/5/2008	-3.17	9/5/2008	1/2/2009	-25.64
1/2/2009	3/6/2009	-26.73	3/6/2009	3/20/2009	13.45
3/20/2009	N/A *	32.15			
Overall Return = -15%			Overall Return = 94%		

*Through August 31, 2009; past performance does not guarantee future results.

Second Opinion

To further demonstrate this concept, we ran a test where the S&P 500 was purchased anytime it hit a new 21-day high. Using a fixed holding period of one month, the average trade lost close to one percent. Buying the S&P 500 when it hit a 21-day low yielded a better result than buying when it was at a 21-day high.

When analyzing the overall market, you can not use the same techniques that you apply for stocks or sector ETFs. Just as a sports car drives differently than a big SUV, the overall market moves differently than a single growth stock. Buying breakouts works well for stocks and sector ETFs, but not so with the overall market. A stock or sector ETF can enter a strong trend for long periods, but the overall market rarely does.

FOLLOW FINANCE AND CONSTRUCTION

Knowing which sectors have the highest correlation to the market during bullish periods is important. First, this knowledge can be used to help determine the market environment. When the sectors with the highest correlation to the S&P 500 perform well, it indicates a healthy market. Conversely, when those sectors underperform, even when the market is advancing, exercise caution. Second, it helps you determine which sectors to hold in a portfolio. If you believe the market will advance, then you will want to own the sectors that advance with the market.

To determine which sectors show the highest correlation to the market during bullish periods, we found seven bullish periods and then ran a correlation study comparing large sectors to the S&P 500 index on each.

Table 6.2 shows the results of this study. For every period, we ranked each sector from the most highly correlated (a ranking of 1) to the least correlated (a ranking of 13). The table is sorted by the last column, which is an average of all the rankings. Those sectors at the top of the table show the highest correlation to the S&P 500 during bullish environments, while those near the bottom have the lowest correlation.

Examining Table 6.2, we immediately see that finance-related ETFs show the strongest correlation to the market. In fact, the top three sectors are all finance-related.

When the market is advancing, financial sectors should perform well.

Looking at the sectors with the lowest correlation, we see energy and metals and mining. That does not come as a surprise, since these tend to move with their underlying base commodity. The surprise is that telecommunications, a high beta sector, is less dependent on market movement than most of the other sectors.

Armed with this information, we can make several conclusions. When you run price-change reports and see the financial sectors rise to the top, it is a bullish sign for the overall market. When the market is advancing, the financial sectors should do well. Be cautious when they start to falter in a rising market. Since banking and home construction ETFs were the worst

Market Timing

Table 6.2: Correlations of Sectors to the S&P 500 During Up Markets

	12/9/94 to 5/24/96	7/26/96 to 2/14/97	4/11/97 to 8/1/97	1/9/98 to 7/17/98	10/9/98 to 7/16/99	3/07/03 to 3/5/04	7/23/04 to 7/13/07	Average
Banking	3	1	1	1	1	2	2	2
Finance	1	3	2	2	2	1	1	2
Building/ Construction	6	5	6	3	4	6	3	5
Consumer	5	4	4	6	3	8	4	5
Utility	8	2	3	4	8	10	11	7
Aerospace/ Defense	2	6	8	8	12	9	5	7
Semiconductor	4	13	9	7	7	4	10	8
Transportation	9	10	5	11	6	7	7	8
Technology	7	12	10	10	9	3	6	8
Health Care	10	9	7	5	10	12	8	9
Telecomm	11	11	13	9	5	5	9	9
Metals/Mining	13	8	11	12	11	11	13	11
Energy	12	7	12	13	13	13	12	12

David Vomund

performers in 2008, it is easy to see why this was one of the most devastating bear markets.

Finally, during uncertain times, it is best to hold gold or energy, rather than a more traditional sector.

MARKET TOPS

Market tops are easier to identify than market bottoms. That said, identifying and acting on a top is very difficult. Still, it is useful to judge the risk of the market and make appropriate changes to your portfolio.

The best research I have seen covering the characteristics of market tops comes from Paul Desmond of Lowry Research Corporation. His report, "An Exploration of Bull Market Tops," looks at the characteristics of 14 major market tops dating back to 1929. In short, the common characteristic of each top was poor market breadth. Fewer and fewer stocks participate in the market's final advance toward a top. In war terms—the generals lead, but the troops do not follow.

> **More Info**
>
> For more on Desmond's research on market tops, visit www.lowryresearch.com.

Let's see how this works by looking at the March 2000 high. Figure 6.2 displays the S&P 500 along with two indicators calculated on the 1,500 stocks within the S&P 1500 index. The top indicator shows the percentage of stocks that were 20 percent or more off their yearly high. The bottom indicator shows the percentage of stocks within two percent of their yearly highs. Notice that on the day of the market top, only seven percent of the S&P 1500 stocks were within two percent of their yearly highs, while 60 percent of the stocks were already 20 percent or more off their highs. The index may have been at a new high, but most stocks had already entered their bear market.

Figure 6.2

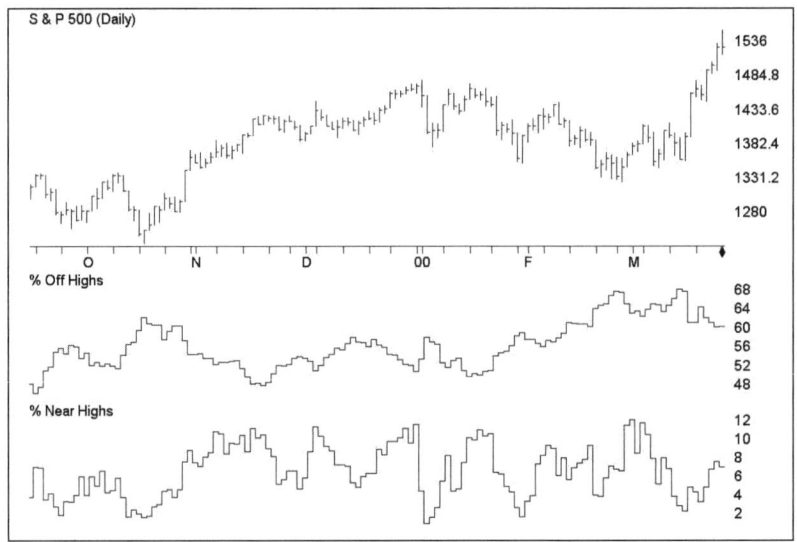

The S&P 500 along with the market breadth indicators. At the March 2000 high, market breadth was very poor. | Courtesy AIQ

During the October 2007 high, the results were less extreme, but still dramatic. Looking at the S&P 1500 stocks, only 22 percent were within two percent their yearly high, while 28 percent had already fallen 20 percent or more off their highs.

From this study, we see the majority of stocks begin to fall before the major market averages do. That means that at the end of bull markets, most investors see their stock and sector ETF portfolios fall in value before the widely followed indexes do.

Advance/Decline Line

The most widely used method of evaluating market participation is to examine the Advance/Decline Line. This market-breadth indicator compares the advancing stocks on the New York Stock Exchange (NYSE) to the declining stocks. When the Advance/Decline Line is stronger than the S&P 500, there is broad market participation and the troops are leading the generals. When the S&P 500 is stronger, however, market breadth is poor, which serves as a warning flag that the stock market risk is increasing. This technical indicator can be found in *Barron's*, *Investor's Business Daily*, and many other publications.

Using the widely published Advance/Decline Line, charts will show deteriorating market participation at major market highs, such as in March 2000 or October 2007. But the commonly used indicator found in major publications does not always represent what is actually happening to the underlying market. That is because nearly half of the NYSE issues are preferred issues, closed-end bond funds, stock funds, ADRs, and warrants. Therefore, while the advancing and declining figures are technically correct, they are misleading because about half of the issues represent "irregular" equities.

The difference can be noticeable. In Figure 6.3, we see the Dow Jones Industrial Average along with the Advance/Decline Line. Using this measurement of market breadth, one would be impressed during the June through August period. While the market was moving lower, the Advance/Decline Line was stair-stepping higher. It implied that the majority of the stocks were advancing. Unfortunately, that was not the case. Figure 6.4 displays our Advance/Decline Line calculated from the price activity of 1,500 com-

Figure 6.3

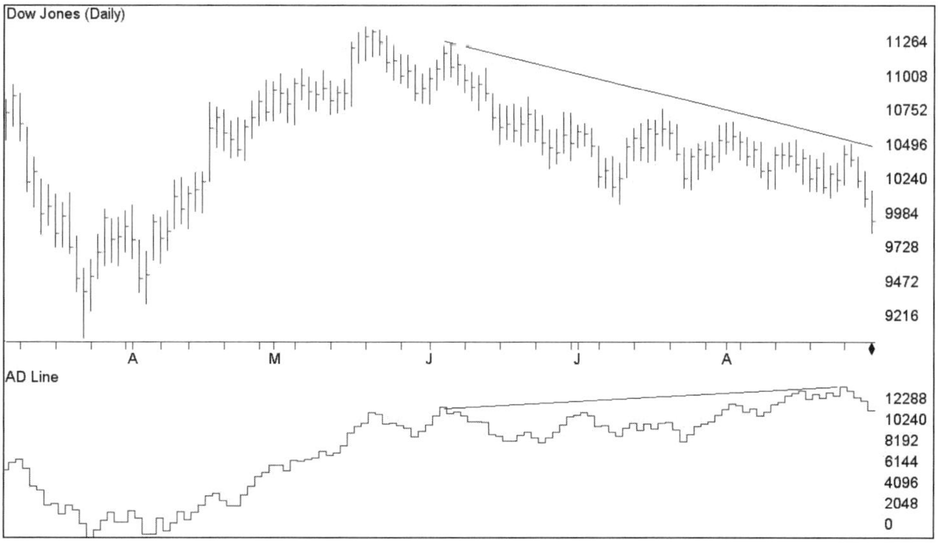

The Dow with the standard Advance/Decline Line. | Courtesy AIQ

mon stocks. This indicator shows a poor investment climate where the majority of stocks were falling.

Figure 6.4

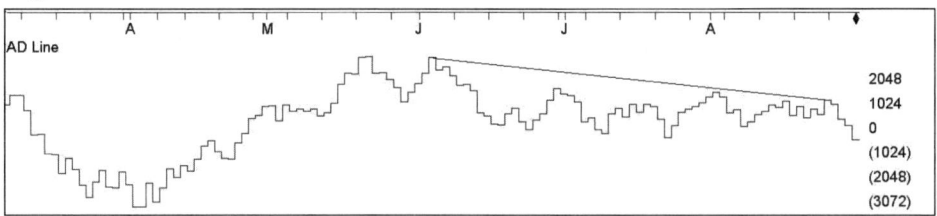

The Dow with an Advance/Decline Line calculated from 1,500 stocks. | Courtesy AIQ

During most periods, the standard Advance/Decline Line will be similar to one calculated from a list of common stocks, but there are times where differences such as the ones we just saw in the last two figures appear. The widely published indicator is sufficient for most people's use, but if you are using market-breadth indicators to identify market tops, then it is best to calculate the data based on a database of common stocks. It makes a difference.

Figure 6.5

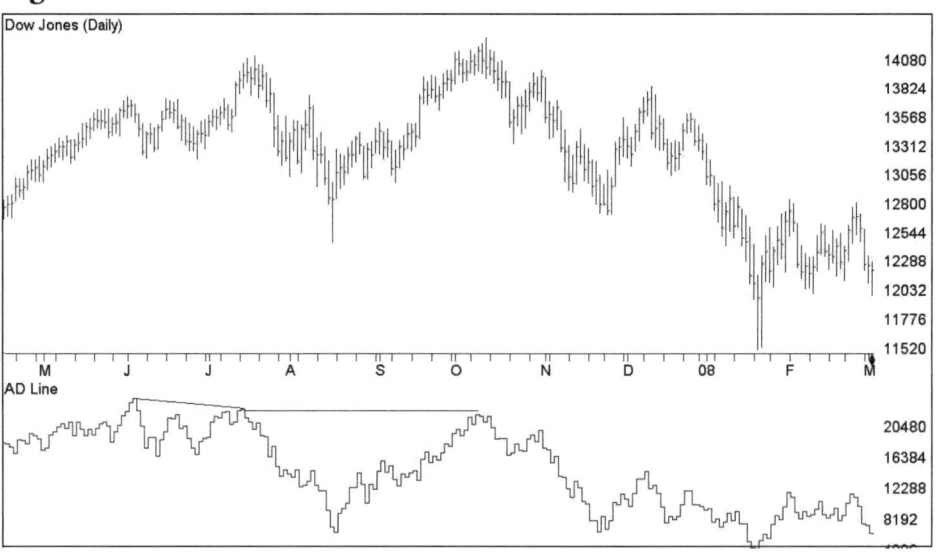

The Dow with the standard Advance/Decline Line at the 2007 market top. | Courtesy AIQ

Consider the important 2007 market top. The commonly used Advance/Decline Line gave a modest warning that the Dow was overstating the health of the market. In Figure 6.5, we see there was a negative divergence in June and July, when the Dow made a new high but the Advance/Decline Line did not. Also, in October, the Dow made a new high—albeit by a small amount—but the Advance/Decline Line was flat.

The negative breadth readings were more pronounced in our calculated Advance/Decline Line (Figure 6.6). This chart shows continued market deterioration from July through October, even when the Dow made a new high. An Advance/Decline Line calculated from a list of common stocks gave more accurate readings.

Figure 6.6

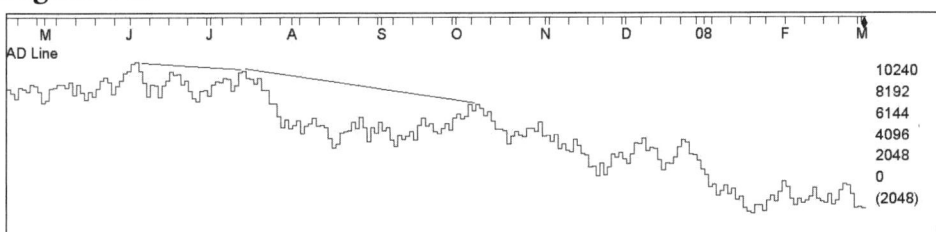

The Dow with the calculated Advance/Decline Line at the 2007 market top. | Courtesy AIQ

MOVING AVERAGE CROSSOVERS

200-Day Moving Average

The 200-day moving average technique—being in the market when S&P 500 is above the moving average and exiting when the market is below—is growing in popularity because this technique served investors well during the early 2000s. Over the first decade or so of the new millennium, there were two large bear markets. Applying a 200-day moving average technique saved many investors from large drawdowns in their portfolios.

That said, even though the 1998 through 2008 period seems perfectly suited to using a 200-day moving average system, one still would have underperformed a buy-and-hold approach, and the majority of trades were losers. Still, this timing system lowers portfolio risk and reduces drawdowns. It has merit.

Reducing Risk

Theodore Wong wrote a thorough article for AdvisorPerspectives.com about the moving average crossover technique. He examined 138 years of stock market data and found the biggest benefit of using a moving average crossover was that it reduced risk. Portfolio drawdowns were far less when employing any moving average system that used monthly charts.

Wong also found that over the past 138 years, the returns were far higher using moving average crossover systems compared to buy-and-hold. That is primarily due to the Great Depression. From 1941 to June 2009, however, the return from market timing using a six-month moving average was about the same as buy-and-hold (although drawdown was less). The bottom line is that a moving average crossover system does not necessarily beat the market. Like other timing models, a moving average system is not necessary in a bull market, but it can greatly reduce portfolio drawdowns in the rare but painful bear markets.

Using a moving average crossover system can significantly reduce portfolio drawdowns during a bear market.

NASDAQ RSMD MODEL

When you use trend lines and 200-day moving averages for your market timing, you are using techniques that many others use as well. To gain an edge, it is helpful to incorporate some form of analysis that is unique; something that will help you determine market direction in a more informed manner. My favorite of these unique techniques is to look at the Nasdaq Composite's relative strength versus the S&P 500.

The Nasdaq is like a mood ring for the market. The Nasdaq stocks tend to be more volatile and aggressive than the blue-chip stocks represented in the S&P 500. When big-money players like the market, they move money to the Nasdaq stocks because of their better growth potential. When they are nervous, however, investors prefer the safety of the less volatile S&P 500 index.

In my studies, I have found that the most favorable market environments occur when the Nasdaq Composite outperforms the S&P 500. That is true even if you do not own Nasdaq stocks.

To quantify this analysis and give actual buy and sell signals, let me introduce the weekly RSMD indicator. RSMD stands for Relative Strength using the MACD indicator. When the common relative strength indicator is plugged into the MACD formula, we get an indicator that measures the momentum of relative strength. Weekly data is used to reduce the number of signals and thereby get the major trends. The RSMD formula is found in Table 6.3.

When the RSMD indicator favors the Nasdaq over the S&P 500, people are willing to take more aggressive positions and the market is generally more favorable. When the indicator favors the S&P 500 over the Nasdaq, money has moved to more conservative stocks and the market is generally unfavorable. Rather than waiting for a crossover of the two lines as we did earlier in this chapter, we are simply looking at the direction of the price phase line—the faster of the two lines. Anytime this line reverses directions, it represents a buy or sell signal.

Let's explain this concept with the aid of a graph. In Figure 6.7, we plot the Nasdaq Composite's weekly RSMD indicator relative to the S&P 500. When the indicator's fast line is rising, then the Nasdaq Composite is outperforming the S&P 500, making for a more bullish environment.

A market-timing buy signal using the RSMD indicator occurs when the fast line of this indicator ticks higher after being in a downtrend. It then remains on a buy until the fast line moves lower. In Figure 6.7, we see the indicator was moving lower from January through April 2005. The Nasdaq was underperforming, so investors were unwilling to own volatile growth stocks in that market environment. By May, however, investors' market opinion improved to where they were willing to take on more risk. It was a much more favorable market environment. Since this is a weekly indicator, signals are not known until after Friday's close.

Table 6.3: RSMD Formula

Signal Line (SL):
$$SL = s_3 DL + (1 - s_3) SL_{t-1}$$

Differential Line (DL):
$$DL = Ra1 - Ra2$$
$$Ra1_t = s_1 R_t + (1 - s_1) Ra1_{t-1}$$
$$Ra2_t = s_2 R_t + (1 - s_2) Ra2_{t-1}$$

Relative Strength (R):

$$R_t = \frac{\left(\dfrac{Pc_t}{Ic_t}\right)}{RSF}$$

$$RSF = \left(\frac{Pc_0}{Ic_0}\right) 100$$

Where:

SL	=	Signal Line
DL	=	Differential Line
$Ra1$	=	Short-term Average Relative Strength
$Ra2$	=	Long-term Average Relative Strength
R_t	=	Relative Strength, day t
Pc_t	=	Closing Price, day t
Ic_t	=	Index closing price, day t
RSF	=	Relative Strength Factor
R	=	Relative Strength
Pc_0	=	Closing Price, day t_0
Ic_0	=	Index closing price, day t_0
s_1	=	Smoothing constant one
s_2	=	Smoothing constant two
s_3	=	Smoothing constant three
t_0	=	First date with data for ticker and index

Figure 6.7

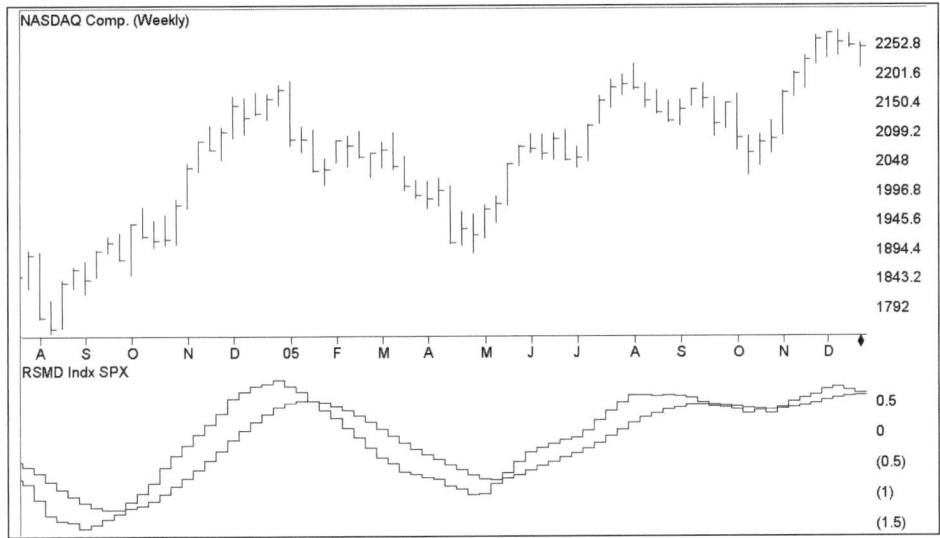

The weekly Nasdaq Composite along with its relative strength versus the S&P 500 (RSMD SPX) indicator. | Courtesy AIQ

To test this indicator, we purchased the S&P 500 index during periods when the Nasdaq Composite outperformed (i.e., indicator moves higher) and then moved to cash during times when the S&P 500 outperformed (i.e., indicator moves lower). The reason we purchased the S&P 500 instead of the Nasdaq Composite is because we were testing for market timing and the S&P 500 is a better measure of the entire market.

The trade-by-trade results are found in Table 6.4. Using a one-week reversal technique, we see that the Nasdaq Composite's RSMD indicator was moving lower until February 16, 1996, the week the indicator rose in value. We purchased the S&P 500 using that day's closing price and held it until June 7, 1996. June 7 represents the day that the indicator had its first decrease in value. Funds were moved to the money market on that day.

Table 6.4: Trade Details During Times When the Nasdaq Outperforms the S&P 500

Buy Date	Sell Date	SPX %Ch.
2/16/1996	6/7/1996	3.91
8/30/1996	10/18/1996	9.03

Table 6.4: Trade Details During Times When the Nasdaq Outperforms the S&P 500

Buy Date	Sell Date	SPX %Ch.
12/6/1996	12/20/1996	1.25
1/3/1997	2/7/1997	5.55
4/11/1997	4/18/1997	3.89
5/2/1997	6/13/1997	9.88
6/20/1997	7/4/1997	2.03
7/11/1997	10/17/1997	3.00
1/23/1998	3/20/1998	14.78
3/27/1998	4/10/1998	1.39
4/17/1998	5/22/1998	-1.09
6/26/1998	8/21/1998	-4.58
9/25/1998	10/2/1998	-4.03
10/30/1998	2/19/1999	12.79
4/2/1999	4/16/1999	1.96
6/25/1999	8/6/1999	-1.14
8/27/1999	10/22/1999	-3.46
11/5/1999	3/17/2000	6.87
6/9/2000	7/28/2000	-2.54
8/25/2000	9/8/2000	-0.79
1/12/2001	2/9/2001	-0.27
3/23/2001	3/30/2001	1.80
4/13/2001	8/17/2001	-1.82
10/12/2001	1/25/2002	3.82
3/8/2002	3/15/2002	0.16
5/17/2002	5/24/2002	-2.06
7/12/2002	7/26/2002	-7.44
8/16/2002	8/30/2002	-1.37
9/6/2002	10/4/2002	-10.44
10/11/2002	12/20/2002	7.24
12/27/2002	1/3/2003	3.79
1/10/2003	1/17/2003	-2.78

Table 6.4: Trade Details During Times When the Nasdaq Outperforms the S&P 500

Buy Date	Sell Date	SPX %Ch.
1/24/2003	1/31/2003	-0.66
2/14/2003	3/28/2003	3.43
4/17/2003	5/23/2003	4.43
5/30/2003	8/8/2003	1.45
8/22/2003	9/26/2003	0.38
10/3/2003	10/17/2003	0.92
11/7/2003	11/14/2003	-0.27
1/9/2004	1/30/2004	0.83
4/2/2004	4/16/2004	-0.63
4/23/2004	4/30/2004	-2.92
6/18/2004	6/25/2004	-0.05
7/9/2004	9/10/2004	1.00
1/7/2005	5/6/2005	-1.25
8/26/2005	9/2/2005	1.07
10/21/2005	10/28/2005	1.59
11/4/2005	12/16/2005	3.86
1/6/2006	1/20/2006	-1.86
1/27/2006	2/3/2006	-1.53
3/31/2006	4/21/2006	1.27
8/18/2006	12/15/2006	9.58
1/5/2007	1/19/2007	1.48
2/23/2007	3/2/2007	-4.41
4/6/2007	4/20/2007	2.81
4/27/2007	5/11/2007	0.79
6/1/2007	8/17/2007	-5.88
8/31/2007	9/14/2007	0.70
9/28/2007	11/9/2007	-4.78
3/28/2008	7/3/2008	-3.98
7/11/2008	8/29/2008	3.50
10/10/2008	10/17/2008	4.60

Table 6.4: Trade Details During Times When the Nasdaq Outperforms the S&P 500

Buy Date	Sell Date	SPX %Ch.
12/12/2008	5/8/2009	5.63
6/5/2009	7/31/2009	5.04

Table 6.5: Summary Statistics (January 1, 1996 - July 31, 2009)

S&P 500 Overall % Return When the S&P Outperforms	S&P Overall % Return When the Nasdaq Outperforms	Round-Trip Trades Per Year
-20	98	9

Table 6.5 shows the all-important summary statistics. The period of our testing was from January 1996 through July 2009 and includes both bull and bear markets. If you owned the S&P 500 index only when the Nasdaq was outperforming (i.e., the weekly RSMD was rising), you would have made 99 percent. If, however, you owned the S&P 500 only when the S&P 500 was outperforming, you would have lost 20 percent. Although past performance does not guarantee future results, the results confirm that the market is more favorable when the Nasdaq outperforms the S&P 500.

> *The market is more favorable when the Nasdaq outperforms the S&P 500.*

It should be noted that being out of the market from August 29, 2008 to October 10, 2008 greatly improved the overall statistics; but I have written about and followed this system since 2001, so the system was not back-fitted to make it work. Even without that one trade, the results were favorable.

CONCLUSION

Invest in the market when it is advancing and sit on the sidelines when it is declining. Who would not want to do that? Unfortunately, it is easier said than done, which is the reason that many people do not attempt to time the market. It is very hard to outperform the market by market timing, but periodically moving to cash does lower a portfolio's risk. For that reason, market timing can play a role in some people's portfolios.

In my market-timing decisions, I try to follow one simple but highly effective rule when making decisions—you can be wrong, but do not be wrong for long. Bad things happen when you are wrong for a long time. Those who are wrong for long periods of time are stubborn with their market opinions. Instead of listening to the market, these people try to tell the market what it should do. Unfortunately, the market is always right.

You can be wrong, but do not be wrong for long.

Quick Quiz

1) What is the benefit of using a 200-day moving average for market timing?

   a. Lower volatility

   b. Increased return

   c. Lower volatility and increased return

2) Buying a market when it first hits a new near-term high or selling the market when it first hits a new near-term low is a good strategy.

   a. True

   b. False

3) If the _____ sector is one of the best performers, it is a bullish sign for the overall market.

   a. health care

   b. consumer

   c. energy

   d. banking

4) Most people's portfolios will top out _____ a bear market begins.

   a. before

   b. at the same time that

   c. after

For the answers to this quiz, please visit the Trader's Library Education Corner online at www.TradersLibrary.com/TLEcorner.

7 Portfolio Management

In this book, we have revealed several very profitable trading strategies. Chapter 5 covered an aggressive growth strategy that was backtested on stocks. From 1999 through 2005 (the period during which the strategy performed best), the average annual rate of return was an amazing 39 percent. Sound enticing? Unfortunately, most people would never see that return. That is because starting in May 2002, the system had nine losing trades to one winning trade. In just three months, the portfolio lost nearly one third of its value. Could you withstand that drawdown? If you started trading the system at the start of the drawdown, how would you feel?

In Chapter 2, our Tactical Allocation model had positive returns in all but one year. Its 17 percent annual return was exceptional, especially given that the market was flat over the same period. Yet there were two occasions when portfolio values plunged by 20 percent. Could you withstand that drawdown? If you invested in the system at the start of the drawdown, how would you feel? Would you have stopped trading it?

These are important questions. A good trading system is only profitable if you are able to stick with it. People never exit a risky system after a highly profitable period; they always exit a system after its worst period, thereby locking in the losses.

A good trading system is only profitable if you are able to stick with it.

Adding insult to injury, people often begin investing in a trading system right before its drawdown period. As a money manager, I see how easy it is to get new clients after a good market run and how hard it is to open new accounts when stocks have fallen.

I would like to say that we could tweak trading systems to eliminate drawdown periods without hurting the upside results, but that is not doable. Every highly profitable system requires risk-taking.

The best way to ensure that you stick with a trading system is to place the proper amount of funds to that strategy. The 20 percent drawdown in our Tactical Allocation approach would be extremely uncomfortable if you placed your entire investment portfolio in the strategy, but it is far more comfortable and easier to live with if you placed 10 percent of your portfolio in the strategy.

Using the common pyramid analogy, the most aggressive trading programs are typically at the top of the pyramid, representing a small portion of your overall portfolio. An approach that uses more diversified ETFs, such as style index ETFs, can represent a larger portion of a portfolio and thus would be in the middle of the pyramid. The majority of an investment portfolio is typically placed in a more conservative model that has a lower volatility level, produces some income, and allows the investor to sleep well at night. For this bottom section of the investment pyramid, a Volatility Managed Portfolio is a great approach.

VOLATILITY MANAGED PORTFOLIOS™

Depending on your risk tolerance, a portion of your overall investment portfolio can be placed into growth strategies, such as those covered in this book. The investments for the remainder of the portfolio should be more diversified and the funds managed in a way that allows for growth, but without the volatility that forces investors to run for the exits after a big market drop. That is where the innovative concept of Volatility Managed Portfolios comes in.

My good friend and colleague Thomas Hardin of Canterbury Investment Management (www.canterburygroup.com) developed Volatility Managed Portfolios™. Tom has more than 30 years of investment experience and is both a Certified Financial Planner (CFP) and a Certified Market Technician (CMT). I interviewed Tom in the fall of 2009 to learn more about his portfolio management ideas and his Volatility Managed Portfolios technique.

Vomund: Tom, what is portfolio management and what is the benefit of practicing portfolio management principles?

Hardin: Many investors believe that taking on more risk should lead to a greater return on investment. Modern Portfolio Theory, first introduced by Nobel Prize winner Harry Markowitz, states that one can generate a higher return with less portfolio fluctuation when the investments in one's portfolio work together. Modern Portfolio Theory shifted attention away from the individual securities and toward the composition of the portfolio as a whole. One of the basics behind this theory is the attempt to create an efficient portfolio, one that earns the highest return with the least amount of volatility. This may be accomplished by owning a diverse group of securities that fluctuate independently from one another.

The key to portfolio management and proper diversification is all about managing market risk. There are plenty of opportunities to make money in the markets. The mission of a good portfolio manager is to avoid large declines during difficult market cycles.

Vomund: Modern Portfolio Theory and risk management sound good in theory. The truth is that most portfolio managers, including those who had highly diversified portfolios, took a bath during 2008 and the first part of 2009. What happened to the "benefit of diversification"?

Hardin: Good question. Most risk management models introduced by academia and embraced by Wall Street simply do not work when they are needed most! I am talking about traditional diversification models, portfolio optimization programs based on the bell curve and Monte Carlo simulation, fixed asset allocation strategies based on age or risk tolerance, and indexing (buying and holding securities that simulate market indexes, like the S&P 500).

Traditional methods are based on math equations that are better suited for estimating the likelihood of flipping a coin to get five heads in a row. Harry Markowitz said that predicting the most efficient portfolio requires predicting future correlation and future returns. Now there is a catch-22.

Most risk management models rely too much on historical investment returns and relationships among various securities. These theories predict risk based on the bell-shaped curve and normal distribution. The bell curve is great for predicting things like the probabilities of variation in height in America (I don't think you will find many twenty-foot-tall people), but not so much for the stock market.

Long-term stock market returns are dominated by low-probability events. Remember in the late 1990s when the Nobel laureates at Long-Term Capital Management almost caused a collapse that jeopardized the financial system? Their flawed traditional math model gave an "almost" impossible probability of something going wrong. The problem is that these "unlikely events" occur with much more regularity than math models would predict. The inability to manage the unlikely and sometimes devastating effects of volatility in the stock market requires an entirely different approach.

Vomund: So what did we learn from the bear markets of 2000 through 2002 and 2007 through 2009, and what can we do to protect ourselves during difficult times?

Hardin: We learned that traditional Wall Street investment strategies are stagnant and do not work during volatile markets. The truth is that Wall Street firms could not manage their own or their clients' risk. Wall Street's risk management models are based on probabilities from efficient markets and normal fluctuations. Inefficient and highly volatile markets, like those of 2008, are caused by emotional investors reacting to unexpected events. Traditional "value at risk" models are rendered worthless.

Many investors believed an asset allocation of 70 percent large stocks and 30 percent Treasuries represented a conservative strategy. Such an allocation combined with a traditional buy-and-hold strategy led to more than a 400 percent increase in volatility and over a 30 percent decline in the value during 2008. Periodic rebalancing to the original allocation fared even worse, and investors learned:

- High-market volatility can negate decades of growth and savings.

- When risk management fails, investors have little or no chance of meeting their goals.

- Risk management methods must be as dynamic as the market's changing volatility.

The markets are dynamic and always changing. To be successful, one must employ investment and risk management processes that are at least as dynamic as the market itself.

Vomund: Do you use global diversification to reduce risk?

Hardin: Yes, I do use ETFs and American Depository Receipts to invest outside the United States. Global investing can add a layer of diversification in normal market environments but can only add little, if any, benefit in highly volatile stock markets.

The changing market volatility is similar to the changing outdoor temperature. To keep your home comfortable, you use a thermostat to manage your indoor temperature. Like the thermostat in your home, your asset allocation and diversification process should adjust to maintain a consistent and comfortable level of volatility in your portfolio. The markets are increasingly dynamic. We need to look beyond traditional risk management methods to manage today's unprecedented volatility.

Here are some simple points to note.

1. Portfolios should include more asset classes than just traditional stocks. Stock market volatility changes over time. For example, the volatility of the S&P 500 more than doubled from 2008 to 2009. The effect of doubling the market's volatility on an equity portfolio that is 50 percent invested is that it fluctuates as though it were 100 percent invested. The result of "fixed" asset allocation is variable and uncontrolled volatility—or risk!

2. Ask yourself, "what am I tracking?" What are the important changes that could have a negative effect on your investments? This is particularly important in today's market, where investors are looking for the best ways to manage risk.

3. Measure portfolio risk. One powerful (and free) tool is RiskGrades (www.RiskGrades.com). This site assists investors in analyzing the risk of their current portfolio.

4. Keep a keen eye on all investments. Think businesslike and keep a sell mindset. But do not overreact to the daily ups and downs on Wall Street. Most of the time, Wall Street offers several excuses in a day for these ups and downs.

5. Think outside traditional Wall Street methods. Academic types study risk management methods including asset allocation, diversification, and modern portfolio theory. Many of these traditional systems are just too static to adjust to the dynamics of today's financial markets. Many investment professionals believe asset allocation (percent of cash, bonds, and stock in a portfolio) should remain the same over time. Changing a portfolio's allocation can be considered to be "market timing."

Vomund: Can you give me an example of a common risk management myth and what to do to avoid making a mistake?

Hardin: A good example of a risk management myth is the investment industry's false belief that a portfolio's asset allocation should always remain about the same. In other words, if a portfolio is allocated 70 percent stocks and 30 percent bonds, the common belief is that making a change in allocation is considered to be an attempt to time the market.

Timing the market is defined as the attempt to have more money invested in the market when the market is going up and less in when it is going down. Buying low and selling high would be a great accomplishment, but most people do the opposite. The tendency is to be optimistic at peaks, causing many investors to add money at the high. They then get pessimistic at the bottom of the cycle and sell close to the bottom.

So if making tactical changes in asset allocation is market timing, then employing a buy-and-hold or fixed asset allocation strategy should be the opposite of market timing, right? Wrong. The truth is, the traditional strategy of buying and holding or maintaining a fixed asset allocation is actually the same as timing the market 100 percent backward every time!

Let me explain. A buy-and-hold or fixed asset allocation strategy will result in variable money or dollar value of an investment. The key words in my definition of market timing are "variable money." When asset allocation is fixed, the amount of money or value of the investment will always be larger at the peaks and smaller at the bottoms. If one were to buy-and-hold a stock or fund, the asset allocation would be fixed. As a result, if $1,000 was invested at a peak in price and then it fell 50 percent, that investment would be worth only $500. A 50 percent decline would require a 100 percent (not 50 percent) advance to get the $500 back to the $1,000 break-even point.

A buy-and-hold or fixed asset allocation strategy accomplishes the opposite of the desired result. When a fluctuation in value occurs, not making an offsetting adjustment in the allocation or position size would have the same effect as timing the market badly.

Vomund: Interesting. Buying and holding a fluctuating asset has the same effect as market timing. What impact does the changing market volatility have on our investment process?

Hardin: Changing market volatility magnifies the negative effects of a buy-and-hold strategy. When the market's volatility doubles, a fully invested equity portfolio feels like it is on leverage. High market volatility is associated with bear markets. We have a choice to maintain a consistent asset allocation by doing nothing, rebalancing to the original allocation from time to time, or focusing on maintaining consistent portfolio volatility. If we opt for consistent volatility, tactical adjustments in asset allocation must be made as the portfolio's volatility increases or decreases.

Each investor has his or her own comfort zone in terms of volatility. The volatility comfort zone can be maintained by a tool developed here at Canterbury called the Portfolio Thermostat™. As investments get more volatile (i.e., heat up), tactics are used to cool the portfolio down to where it is comfortable. As volatility declines (i.e., cools off), we make adjustments to heat the portfolio back up.

The end result of managing a portfolio's volatility within a narrow range is that it acts like a ratchet and benefits from the up and down swings of the market. When the market goes down, the portfolio should decline less. When the market rebounds, the portfolio should advance from a higher base. That is far different than maintaining a fixed asset allocation, where volatility (i.e., risk) is variable and uncontrolled.

Vomund: The Portfolio Thermostat approach was harder to implement before the development of ETFs.

Hardin: The world of ETFs is getting very interesting. One can own ETFs in hard and soft commodities, currencies, real estate, long and inverse market indexes, or entire sectors and industries. We can even own volatility itself through the S&P 500 Volatility Index ETF.

Again, technological advances have revolutionized how we measure and manage risk. RiskGrades can be used to calculate the risk of the components of a portfolio and the risk of the portfolio as a whole, which is the first step in managing risk. RiskGrades gives a better understanding of the level of risk and how much a portfolio is benefiting from diversification.

Inverse ETFs are a very important tool in the Portfolio Thermostat process. When the market's volatility heats up (i.e., the market declines rapidly), we need something to cool it down to our comfort zone. One tool investors can use in such an environment is an inverse ETF. Inverse ETFs hold securities that go in the opposite direction of their equivalent market index, such as the S&P 500. They can be used to lower portfolio risk during highly volatile times. Inverse funds can also be used to make money when the market goes down because these funds go up, creating a possibility for the portfolio manager to benefit from declines in the market.

The world continues to become more complex and more competitive. Change is happening at a breakneck pace. Risk management is more important and more difficult than ever. It has been Wall Street's and investors' inability to manage risk that has contributed to the damage to their financial futures over the past few years.

The lesson is this: rather than avoid risk entirely, the revolutionary investor should avoid taking poorly understood risks and instead choose risks whose potential upside justifies the potential downside—or, better yet, learn to benefit from fluctuation.

Vomund: Thank you for sharing your thoughts with us.

> **More Info**
>
> Tom Hardin is the author of *Investor Revolution: Overthrow Wall Street and Take Back Your Future*. For a complimentary copy, please visit www.canterburygroup.com.

CLIMATE CONTROL

Tom Hardin's Portfolio Thermostat approach makes a lot of sense, and his temperature analogy is easy to understand. Just as heaters and air conditioners are used to keep a home's temperature within a comfortable range, tools can be used to keep a portfolio's volatility in a comfortable range.

Keeping your investments within a comfortable range is critical. When fluctuations become too high, people get anxious and make bad decisions. When volatility is too low, it can be hard to make money. In late 2008 and early 2009, volatility was exceptionally high, so investors felt the heat of the market's fluctuations. It was as if the buy-and-holders had three times as much invested. Along the same lines, investors felt the market's chill in 2006 when volatility was very low.

Here is an analogy for how volatility is managed. Let's say the market temperature begins at 150 degrees (high volatility). After some time, the market temperature drops to only 50 degrees (low volatility). In other words, the stock market began with three times the volatility with which it ended.

That means an investor whose assets were in 33 percent stocks and 67 percent cash when the temperature was 150 degrees had the same volatility as an investor with 100 percent stocks when the volatility in the market was 50 degrees.

The goal of the Portfolio Thermostat is to keep the fluctuations in a portfolio within a narrow and predictable range. Let's assume the volatility goal for a portfolio is 50. If the S&P 500's volatility reaches 150, then the portfolio should be 33 percent invested in an index fund and 67 percent invested in the money market. Cash has no volatility, so the third that is invested brings the portfolio volatility to 50 (150 × 0.33).

Now, suppose the market's volatility drops to 25. For the portfolio volatility to remain at 50, we would invest the entire portfolio in a double-leveraged index fund. This is an extreme example, but there are times that a portfolio utilizes a leveraged long fund to reach the desired goal.

> **More Info**
>
> To calculate market volatility and risk, websites such as www.RiskGrades.com offer online tools that can be used.

In each of these two cases, the Portfolio Thermostat adjusts the heat on the portfolio to give it a better chance of obtaining a reasonable return without creating excessive fluctuation.

To calculate the market's volatility, Tom uses the nifty RiskGrades web site. It can calculate risk on the market, individual securities, or a portfolio.

For my own work, I use a standard deviation calculation. Specifically, I use a 21-day exponential moving average of standard deviation. The formula is found in Figure 7.1.

This indicator is a measure of the fluctuation in price over a specified period of time. The calculation is similar to the Standard Deviation formula, which measures dispersion around the mean for a series of values. In the Volatility formula, deviation from the mean is replaced by an exponential function of the change in price from the prior day's (or week's) value. To allow relative comparisons, the Volatility coefficient is expressed as an annualized percentage change.

Figure 7.1

$$V = 100 \sqrt{\frac{Af}{(n-1)} \left[\sum dp^2 - \frac{(\sum dp)^2}{n} \right]}$$

summations for prior periods n through 1

$$dp = \ln\left(\frac{P_t}{P_{t-1}}\right)$$

Where:
  V = Volatility
  Af = Annualization factor (52 for weekly, 250 for daily)
  dp = Log of change in price from prior period
  P_t = Closing Price on day t
  n = Number of periods

21-day exponential moving average of standard deviation.

Divide that value by 0.2 to get the final number in a range that corresponds to Tom's thermostat analogy.

In Figure 7.2, we see how this strategy works. The top chart is the S&P 500, while the bottom chart is the volatility indicator calculated from the formula in Figure 7.1. We have drawn horizontal lines on the indicator to represent a comfort zone, an area where the "temperature" reading was between 70 and 90. When the S&P 500 was within the comfort zone, the portfolio was fully invested.

Figure 7.2

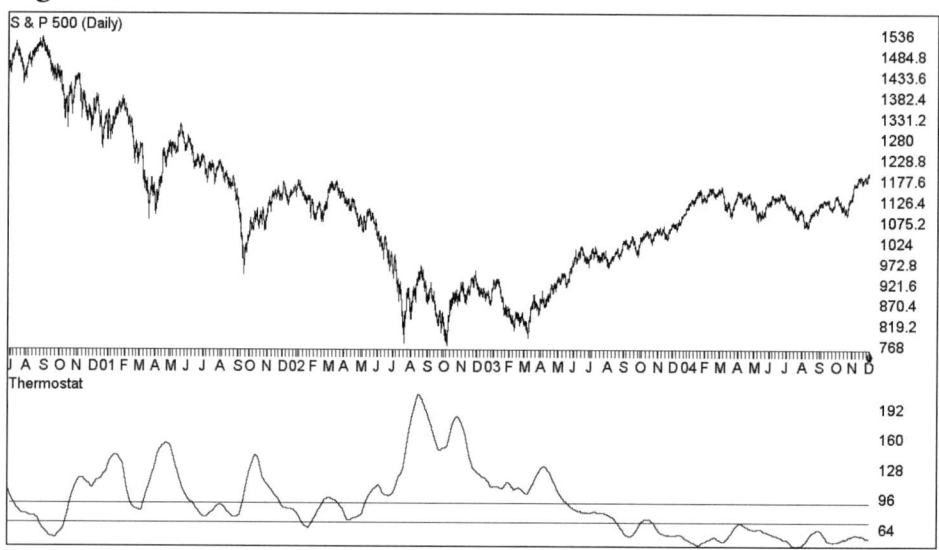

S&P 500 on top, Portfolio Thermostat on the bottom. The horizontal bands represent the comfort zone. | Courtesy AIQ

When the Thermostat was above the range, then cash was raised or an inverse ETF was purchased. Notice that for most of the first half of the chart, the market was falling and volatility was above the comfort range. In May 2001, the Thermostat reached 155, so a portfolio would have to be about 50 percent invested to remain within the comfortable range (80 / 155 = 0.52).

When the indicator is below the range, then a leveraged long ETF should be held. This was the case for much of 2004. By following these actions, the portfolio's overall volatility remained within a comfortable range.

The goal of the Portfolio Thermostat is to keep the fluctuations in a portfolio within a narrow and predictable range.

Outperforming the Market to Increase Returns

Notice that we have not said anything about outperforming the market. While there are many periods where this approach does outperform; that is not the goal. This approach is for comfort. It is about making sure you do not capitulate at a market's low point and making sure your portfolio is not devastated in bear markets.

There are ways, however, to incorporate this approach with a market-timing system to increase returns. This is most easily accomplished by changing the target comfort range depending on market conditions. For example, if the S&P 500 is above its 50-day and 200-day moving averages, the Thermostat target range can be between 70 and 90. If the S&P 500 is below at least one of these moving averages, then the Thermostat target would drop to between 50 and 70.

This approach can also be used in conjunction with strategies that buy sector ETFs, country ETFs, or even stocks. For example, the approach can be combined with our style index strategy from Chapter 2. If the strategy says that iShares Emerging Markets (EEM) and the Nasdaq 100 (QQQQ) should be held, then volatility is measured for each security and partial positions are held when the volatility is too high.

As of this writing, EEM has a Thermostat reading of 110, so a three-quarters position would be held to hit a target of 80. The QQQQ has a Thermostat reading of 80, so a full position can be held. If you hold several securities that do not move in tandem, then the portfolio's Thermostat will be lower than an average of the individual holdings because of a diversification benefit. That is why Tom Hardin runs his RiskGrades calculations on both the individual securities and the overall portfolio.

SELL-SIDE RESEARCH

When you watch the financial channels on TV, you hear a lot about securities to buy. People often focus exclusively on the "when to buy" side of the equation and ignore the sell side. In this section, we will turn this on its head by using a generic entry system and then testing various sell strategies.

Whether you use the mechanical strategy found in Chapter 2 or trade ETFs based on chart pattern and indicator readings, you will need to make sell-side decisions.

In our mechanical strategies chapter, our models included buy and sell decisions. Our relative strength model bought when relative strength was strong and sold when it faltered. Still, I find many people like the model, but they are more comfortable adding additional sell rules in an attempt to limit drawdowns.

Similarly, if you enter ETFs based on chart patterns and indicator readings, you must also have a sell discipline. Most investors are good at limiting losses. Letting a small loss turn into a big loss is devastating, and most people do not let that happen. Traders often do not have a plan, however, when they have a profitable position. "Letting your profits run" is a good maxim, but all too often the security does not run and it is sold after it falls back to its entry point. Testing shows that it is better to lock in the profit than to let the security run with the hope that it turns into a big winner.

Testing the Theory

To demonstrate this point, we created a very generic sector ETF entry system that screens for ETFs that have risen above their 21-day moving average. We used a large list of sector, commodity, and international region ETFs to get more trading signals, thereby making the results more statistically valid. Nearly every ETF, whether it is in an uptrend or downtrend, rises above its 21-day moving average many times throughout a year, so there are a lot of trades. The testing period was January 2003—a time when many sector ETFs were brought to the market—through September 2009.

The entry system is generic, but we test various exit systems. The first test uses a 93 percent trailing stop. This stop system moves to a sell anytime an ETF falls 7 percent from its high point after it is purchased. The trailing stop effectively cuts losses short and lets profits run. As long as the ETF does not pull back 7 percent, traders remain invested, hoping for a parabolic move.

Our test of the 93 percent trailing stop is found in Figure 7.3. There were 1,299 trades with an average holding period of 65 calendar days. The average trade gained 0.76 percent, but the key statistic is the Average Annual ROI of 4.28 percent. That is not the return you will get by using this system, but we can use it for comparison purposes.

Next, let's look at a simple 64 calendar day time stop. We chose 64 days because that was the average holding period from our previous test. Under this sell strategy, you sell the stock after 44 business days (approximately 64 calendar days) no matter how the stock has performed.

The results appear in Figure 7.4. The holding period is the same, and once again, there were about 1,300 trades. This time, however, the Average Annual ROI jumped to 8.41 percent. The fixed holding period was much more effective than the trailing stop exit strategy (in actual trading, you should also employ a capital protect in case you bought at the high).

Our final test uses a profit protect strategy where profits are locked in once a trigger is met. We use a 93 percent capital protect in case we bought the ETF at its high. Once there is an 11 percent profit on the trade, then we lock in 90 percent of that profit (i.e., sell when the holding gives back ten percent of its profit). That way, we do not give back our gains, but we do not immediately sell in case the holding continues to march higher. We chose these numbers because they also lead to a 64-day holding period.

Figure 7.5 shows the results of this new test. The 5.85 percent Average Annual ROI is slightly less than the fixed holding period, but is higher than the trailing stop.

Portfolio Management

Figure 7.3

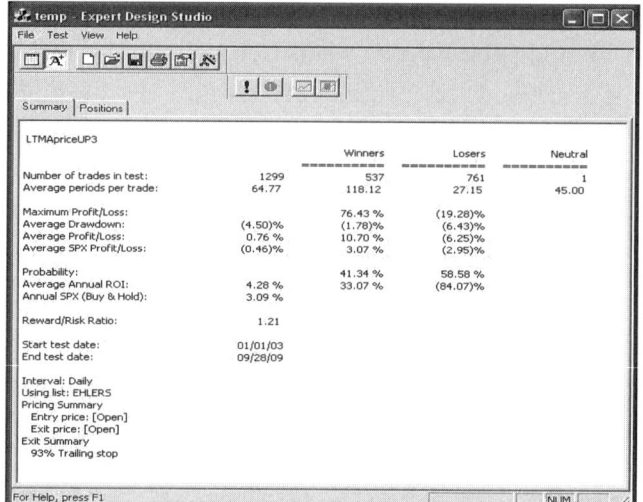

Results using a 93 percent trailing stop.

Courtesy AIQ

Figure 7.4

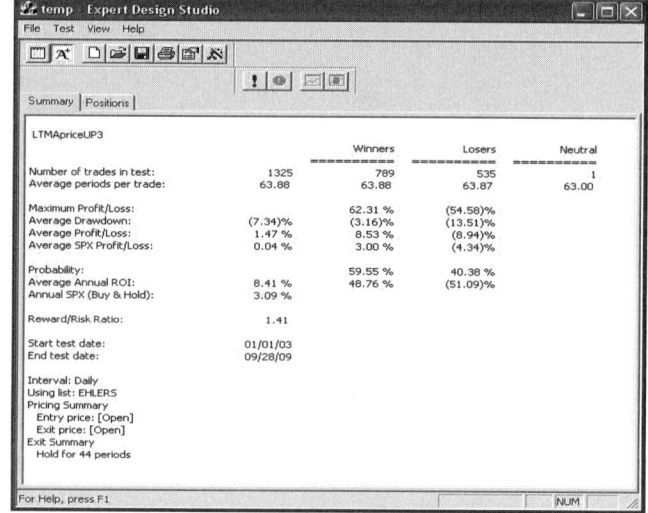

Results using a 64 calendar day holding period.

Courtesy AIQ

Figure 7.5

```
LTMApriceUP3
                                          Winners          Losers          Neutral
                                        ==========      ==========      ==========
Number of trades in test:       1305         620             685              0
Average periods per trade:     63.55        86.77           42.53           0.00

Maximum Profit/Loss:                        38.58 %       (19.28)%
Average Drawdown:             (5.48)%       (2.13)%        (8.52)%
Average Profit/Loss:           1.02 %       11.55 %        (8.52)%
Average SPX Profit/Loss:      (0.08)%        4.71 %        (4.41)%

Probability:                                47.51 %        52.49 %
Average Annual ROI:            5.85 %       48.60 %       (73.10)%
Annual SPX (Buy & Hold):       3.09 %

Reward/Risk Ratio:             1.23

Start test date:             01/01/03
End test date:               09/28/09

Interval: Daily
Using list: EHLERS
Pricing Summary
```

Results using a 93 percent capital protect and a 90 percent profit protect once profits reach 11 percent. |Courtesy AIQ

What does this mean? The trailing stop, designed to keep investors in while the stock moves higher, was the worst performer. That is true for this generic entry system, and it is true for most other entry systems that I have tested. The findings are even more pronounced when tested on individual stocks. Results are more even when tested on diversified ETFs.

Trailing stops keep you invested in securities that go parabolic, but that rarely happens. More often, you get a good profit on a holding, but give back most of that profit before the stop is triggered.

Stop systems that force you to take profits lead to better results. A fixed-period stop system locks in profits because it forces a sell no matter what the security has done. With a fixed-period approach, you must sell an ETF even if it is making a parabolic advance. The profit protect strategy obviously also forces you to lock in profits because it does not allow the holding to move back to its entry point once the profit threshold is reached.

Traders often have a set level that acts as a stop-loss in case the trade does not go as well as expected. They end up locking in losses, but have no plan to lock in gains. This testing shows the importance of having a strategy that does not give profits back.

It is better to lock in the profit than to let the security run with the hope that it turns into a big winner.

FINAL THOUGHTS

When you watch CNBC or read financial publications, you constantly hear analysts giving their buy recommendations. The buy side of investing gets the most attention. Unfortunately, that is only part of the equation. Successful investors are more concerned with portfolio management than simply what to buy.

Without portfolio management, even the most profitable trading systems will lose money. That is because investors will most often leave a trading system after a series of losing trades. The downside volatility becomes too much to bear. With proper portfolio management, portfolio volatility is managed to make a system more comfortable.

One way to become comfortable with a system is to allocate a small portion of your entire portfolio to the model. When large portions of your overall portfolio are used, then the revolutionary Volatility Managed Portfolio concept, where volatility is managed as market environments change, should play a role. Being comfortable with portfolio volatility is key to reaping the rewards of ETF investing.

Quick Quiz

1) What is a Volatility Managed Portfolio?

   a. It is a portfolio that beats the market because one increases exposure when the market is low and reduces exposure when the market is high.

   b. It is a buy and hold portfolio that has a small weighting in an entire portfolio so that an investor is comfortable with its volatility.

   c. It is a portfolio that raises cash or enters leveraged funds in order to maintain a specific volatility level.

2) What is wrong with taking comfort in having a diversified portfolio?

   a. In bad markets, securities become more correlated.

   b. Correlation levels hold steady over time.

   c. In all market environments, there are some areas that will do poorly.

3) What effect does increasing volatility have on buy-and-hold investors?

   a. It gives them an opportunity to add more positions to their portfolio during unwarranted sell-offs.

   b. No effect, because they do not lock in their losses.

   c. It makes a fully invested portfolio feel like it is on leverage.

For the answers to this quiz, please visit the Trader's Library Education Corner online at www.TradersLibrary.com/TLEcorner.

 # Trading Psychology and the Personal Trading Plan

It is easy to see comparisons between winning athletes and successful traders. Think of the Olympics, for example. As difficult as it is for athletes to perform during their events, the really hard work was put in long before the Olympic Games. Swimmers do countless laps to prepare for the games. When we watch the Olympic events, we are seeing the results of each athlete's planning and preparation.

Just as the Olympic athlete can not show up for an event without having done any preparation, neither can an ETF investor. For successful investors, the real effort happens well before entering the trade. Planning and preparing for a successful trade is the hard work; managing the actual trade is the easy part. In this chapter, we will discuss what is required to be a successful trader.

A PERSONAL PROCESS

Those new to trading often think they can buy a great trading book like this one (no modesty here!) and begin trading profitably. It does not work that way. The hardest work needs to come well before you begin to trade. The "just show me the money" crowd does not last long in this industry. Every successful trader has undergone the tedious process of discovering his or her own personal trading strategy.

Developing a personal trading approach takes time and is not easy. You should take concepts from this and other books and then modify and tweak them to fit your style. Run backtests on various systems. The more you test and modify a strategy, the more confidence you will have in the approach and the better it will fit your personality.

CONTROL DESTRUCTIVE EMOTIONS

To profit, it is necessary to risk something. If you risk too much, then emotions take over and you make decisions based on fear. Each trader must learn his or her risk tolerance. Is greed or fear the dominant trait? Those dominated by greed must make sure that they have a solid mechanism to limit portfolio drawdowns. Those who are dominated by fear need to find a confident, positive attitude. Visualize successful trades. You often get what you believe.

Learning to tolerate the uncertainty is essential to success. Sometimes this means staying invested as the market moves lower. The more often you have a drawdown, the more you will be able to accept it. The same is true for selling stocks at a loss. If your ego is too big and it is hard to sell for a loss, then it might be good to have a lot of losses. The more often you sell for a loss, the easier it will be—and the easier it is, the sooner you will get out next time.

HAVE A TRADING PLAN

Do you buy ETFs high, or are you a bottom-fisher? What part of the chart do you like? Where in the cycle of the chart are you likely to buy and sell? Are there certain indicators that you most often use? These are the types of questions that need to be answered when developing a trading plan.

A trading plan describes your approach to trading. It describes when you buy and when you sell. It describes the trading models you use in security selection. It covers position size and includes "when to sell" rules. Well-researched backtests will help answer these questions. Your plan should be in writing, but realize that it will change over time. Successful traders agree, however, that the changes become fewer and fewer as time passes.

CONFIDENCE

Risk-taking requires a certain amount of guts. Some traders gain confidence after successes and then take on more risk. That is good. Confidence is gained from success—when you know what to do in all situations. Once your trading portfolio has steady gains, you will want to play bigger.

Confidence can also be gained from thorough backtesting. If you do not have confidence in a system, then you might abandon it after a few losing trades. Every successful system will have a string of losing trades. If you have thoroughly tested the system, you may be able to take heart in similar periods of losing trades, and be confident that the system will be profitable again.

REVIEW YOUR TRADES

Did you follow your trading plan on the buy and sell sides? Did you get out too fast, or should you have added to a position? If you followed your trading plan but the security was sold for a loss, then it was a good trade. If you made exceptions to your plan, then it was a bad trade—even if the trade was profitable.

By reviewing your trades, you will develop a more disciplined approach. You will also see if your trading plan needs to be adjusted.

It is tempting to enter a trade without a proper plan or with little preparation. Building a trading plan takes time and is not always fun. It is essential for long-term success, however. It helps to improve the consistency of your decisions and your results.

PSYCHOLOGY TESTED BY TURBULENT TIMES

There is a saying, "never confuse brains with a bull market." In a bull market, those without a good trading plan or the emotional discipline to stick with one can still be successful. A bear market, however, reveals the chinks in the armor. During turbulent times, proper trading psychology becomes essential.

Whether during the 1990 bear market, the bull market of 1994, the 2000 to 2002 Nasdaq crash, or the 2007 to 2009 Great Recession, I look back at the decisions that I made and wonder, "what was I thinking?"

Making good decisions during turbulent times is something we all struggle with because it is human nature to let emotions drive decisions. Those who have a good trading psychology were not born that way; they developed it through experience. Those with a poor trading attitude are easy to identify but are usually in no condition to take advice. We all learn from the school of hard knocks. Here is what I have learned as I look back at how I could have better reacted to turbulent times.

Evaluate Your Profile

First, evaluate your risk tolerance and investment time horizon. If you are very risk averse and can not stomach drawdowns, then your trading system should be designed to take only small losses and to be conservative. Similarly, if you might need the money in less than a few years, then your system should incorporate market timing and should avoid large drawdowns. Conservative systems with low volatility should not be expected to make a lot of money during bull markets.

If, however, you have a long time horizon, then your trading strategy can shoot for high returns without focusing too much on risk. After all, if you have a long-term horizon, then a drawdown is only a problem if you lock in the loss by selling into the weakness.

It is important to know your profile and match your investment program to it. Conservative investors who are uncomfortable with the volatility of very aggressive, high-growth portfolios should avoid such programs because they will exit a risky strategy on the first round of weakness, usually locking in significant losses. If you are a conservative investor or have a short time horizon, stick with low-risk strategies.

Stick with a System

As we have previously discussed, all successful traders have a personal trading system. Everyone develops their own system to match their personality and beliefs.

One of the most common mistakes investors make after developing a system is to not stick with it. They find a strategy that works well, but then exit the strategy during bad times and switch to a new strategy. They are constantly one step too late and end up exiting at the low point of each system's drawdown.

This happens when someone does not have confidence in his or her system. There is no substitute for live trading, but performing thorough backtests can often help build confidence in a system. We have shown effective strategies in this book, but you should test them yourself as well, and then tweak them to fit your needs. That is how to build confidence.

Make Decisions Based on Sound Analysis

Trying to eliminate emotion from the decision-making process is something everyone struggles with. When television reporters yell from a noisy floor of the New York Stock Exchange and proclaim how important that day's trading is, you immediately want to place a trade. The reporters stir your emotions. Often, a single glance at a chart puts everything back in perspective. For many, it is best to make buy and sell decisions when the market is closed.

Are you making decisions based on analysis or emotion? If you perform your analysis but then change your decision based on overnight futures activity, then there is a problem. If you become bullish on days when the market advances and turn bearish on days when the market declines, then there is a problem.

Making decisions based on emotion can be a problem for people who are not active traders, as well. If you ignore your system because of an overall bullish or bearish belief, then you are relying on emotion. People who constantly ignore a system's buy signals because in their heart, they feel equities must be in a bear market, are making decisions based on emotion instead of analysis.

Do the Analysis

During poor market periods, people often decide to stop performing the analysis. They rationalize that once the market improves, they will start investing again. This is a recipe for disaster. When the market recovers, these people are caught flat-footed and miss the move.

This was the case for many in March 2009. Pessimism was so rampant that money market assets represented nearly half of the stock market's capitalization. Without warning, the market gained 40 percent without even a six percent pullback.

Remain Independent

The market does its best to prove most people wrong. Consensus opinions rarely work. Financial web sites will have bullish and bearish articles and eye-catching projections from analysts. These opinions should not influence your decision making. Stick with your personal trading process.

Accept Responsibility

Those with big egos make poor traders. If you can not admit to being wrong, you will not last long in this business.

It is human nature to give oneself credit when things go well and then blame others when things go poorly. The success or failure of an investor rests solely on the person who places the trade. This is true when things go well, and it is true when things go poorly. When your system has a winning streak, give yourself credit because you followed the system and pulled the trigger. When things go poorly, you have to accept responsibility as well, especially if you did not follow your system.

Learn from Mistakes

Everybody makes mistakes. The important point is to learn from the mistakes so you do not repeat them. It is a good practice to review your trading decisions, especially during the turbulent market periods. Sometimes good decisions result in losses, and that is fine.

There may be other cases where bad decisions were made. That is when you evaluate why a bad decision was made and how it can be avoided in the future.

IN CONCLUSION

Putting in the time to develop a personal trading process and then having the emotional makeup to follow the system is essential. Our individual trading process must match our personality. We each need to gain confidence in our strategy and understand that all systems go through bad periods. By sticking with our own approach and applying the proper trading attitudes, we can reach our personal trading objectives.

Quick Quiz

1) Why is it important to stick to a well-tested system even when there are losses?

   a. All systems have drawdowns. A good system will work again.

   b. People exit systems after drawdowns, not after gains. Constantly leaving trading systems when they perform poorly leads to large portfolio losses.

   c. All of the above.

2) Why is it important to have a personal trading process?

   a. An investor will have more confidence in an approach that fits his individual needs.

   b. When too many people use a system, it may no longer work.

   c. Traders can adapt their personality to other trading models.

For the answers to this quiz, please visit the Trader's Library Education Corner online at www.TradersLibrary.com/TLEcorner.

Appendix: Two ETF Options Strategies

It is hard to believe how far exchange-traded funds (ETFs) have grown since their inception, but what is even more impressive is how little investors truly know about how they work and how to choose the best one for the job. In the following pages, I will show you why ETFs are the best vehicle for investors and traders alike, how to choose the best ETF, and my favorite strategies for generating income and growth with ETFs.

Before I share my personal perspective on ETF investing and trading, I want to tell you why I decided to contribute to this book. There is no shortage of investing advice available, as is the case with exchange-traded funds. That is why David Vomund's book is so valuable—from the basics to high level trading psychology, he delivers a highly effective piece of work. I am a technical analyst, so his roots in charting are welcomed and appreciated. As you will learn in this appendix, there is one aspect of ETF trading that Vomund does not cover, and luckily it is my forte. As the lead ETF analyst at BigTrends.com, I utilize options on ETFs to reach short-term and long-term goals. I am excited to share with you my favorite strategies using what I consider to be the best investment vehicles available.

Since 1993, exchange-traded funds have provided active investors with a better way to reach their financial goals and in the past five years, ETF growth has created more opportunities to trade just about anything imaginable. As it stands today, there are over 1,000 exchange-traded products

(ETPs) available that provide simple and cost-efficient access to invest in countries, sectors, niche industries, commodities, and more. Exchange-traded funds have advantages over stocks and mutual funds in a variety of ways. Exchange-traded funds are investment vehicles that hold assets that help the overall fund track an index such as the NASDAQ 100 or Japanese Nikkei Index. Let's begin with a comparison between ETFs, stocks, and mutual funds to show you how they stack up against each other.

In Figure A.1, we have a quick comparison that shows the restrictive nature of mutual funds and the higher risk involved with stocks when compared to exchange-traded funds. After digesting the lower cost, higher transparency, and flexibility found in ETFs, it is easy to understand why they are growing so fast.

Figure A.1

Characteristics	Stocks	ETFs	Mutual Funds
Diversification Benefits	✗	✓	✓
Optionable	✓	✓	✗
Transparency	✓	✓	✗
Management Fees	✗	As Low as .07%	Avg 1.4%
12B-1 Fees	✗	Max .07%	Max 1%
Intraday Pricing	✓	✓	✗
Margin Buying	✓	✓	✗
Short Selling	✓	✓	✗
Control over Capital Gains	✓	✓	✗

Security comparison.

CHOOSING THE BEST ETF FOR THE JOB

With the ETF universe expanding every day, it can become a cumbersome task to determine the best ETF for your goal. For example, active investors interested in profiting from a boom in biotechnology have several broad-based biotech ETFs to choose from. So how do you choose the right one?

For the biotech example, let's look at these four ETFs:

- SPDR Biotech ETF (XBI)
- PowerShares Dynamic Biotech & Genome (PBE)
- iShares NASDAQ Biotechnology (IBB)
- Biotech HOLDRs (BBH)

Each of these ETFs is focused on providing investment results in line with a group of biotech companies. To evaluate any group of ETFs on a level playing field, consider the following characteristics:

- Cost (Expense Ratio)
- Fund Holdings (Diversification)
- Average Volume (Liquidity)
- Benchmarked Performance

The process may seem daunting; however, it is essential to making the correct decision. Notice the core differences in the expense ratios, volume, and annualized performance. Obviously, it is best to choose a low expense ratio, but you also need good liquidity (volume) among others. The other essential characteristic that you need to analyze is the top ten holding. In some cases, you may have 50 percent of an ETF invested in only one or two companies. This is the case with the biotech HOLDRs (BBH) ETF; as of this writing, 67 percent of total assets are invested in two companies—Amgen (AMGN) and Gilead Sciences, Inc (GILD). Diversification is a core benefit to ETFs, so if a fund lacks diversity, look elsewhere. In comparison, XBI and IBB do not have any holding over ten percent. In my view, the iShares NASDAQ Biotech

(IBB) ETF is best based on higher liquidity, solid diversification, and good relative performance.

Overall, I look for the following benchmarks to be met in the best exchange-traded funds when trading options. These levels can be relaxed when your holding period is expected to be longer.

- Volume is greater than 500,000 shares per day.
- No holding is greater than 15 percent of fund (less than ten percent is preferable).
- An expense ratio less than its peers (look at category average on Yahoo! Finance).

In Chapter One, Vomund covered the basics of ETFs very well and I want to build on that education with the basics of options. After mastering the basics of ETFs and options, we can move into my strategies, which use both.

ETF OPTIONS BASICS

There are many things to consider when deciding whether or not to trade options. Even if you are familiar with options trading, hopefully a few things in this section will be new to you. Here are the most important things you need to know about options.

- All options have an expiration month. The option will expire at the close of trading on the third Friday of that month. If you are still holding the options at that time, they will expire and be worthless.
- When you trade options, you are buying or selling options contracts. Each options contract controls a block of 100 options on 100 units of the underlying asset. So if the price of a call option is $2.00 and you want to buy 4 contracts, you will pay $800.00 (2*4*100) and with this payment, you will have the right to purchase 400 shares of the ETF.
- There are a variety of different trading strategies for which options can be used. The most basic and probably the most common is simply buying puts and calls. More strategies include selling options, and

using sets of options for calendar spreads, straddles, strangles, and butterflies.

There is much more involved with trading options, but these are some of the most basic concepts to help you fully understand my ETF options strategies.

THE CONCEPT OF "INCOME TRADING"

Let's start with a strategy that works well for options beginners. It is a conservative income strategy using spreads. Many new options traders are seriously intimidated by the idea of owning two options on the same underlying ETF at the same time, and they miss out on all the possible rewards that can come from utilizing options in all of the ways that they can be.

The idea of income trading is not new; people do it every day. The concept is that you hold an asset of some sort. Think of it as a longer-term asset, like a house. But you aren't living in the house, you aren't fully utilizing it, and you want to lower your cost of continuing to own the asset.

What can you do?

I am sure you rapidly came to the idea that you could rent the house to someone else and bring in some cash flow to offset your mortgage payments. This is exactly what income trading is all about. Let's look at the single most common options strategy on earth—the covered call—for a better understanding.

Covered Call Example

Let's say that Mary has 1,000 shares of an ETF that she bought a while ago for $50, and that the ETF hasn't moved at all and has recently been trading for $50.00 per share. Mary considers her alternatives in Table A.1.

I know which outcome I'm rooting for!

Now, obviously the chance of the ETF going to zero is remote—but as we saw in 2008 and again in the "Flash Crash" of 2010, a remote chance does not mean no chance.

Table A.1: ETF Alternatives

	Value	$ Gain	% Change
ETF Skyrockets to $100!	$100,000	$50,000	100%
ETF rallies to $54	$54,000	$4,000	8%
1000 Shares at $50	$50,000	break even	0%
ETF drops to $46	$46,000	($4,000)	8%
ETF imitates a lawn dart and goes to zero	$0	($50,000)	(100%)

The covered call is, as we pointed out in our example above, similar to "taking in a renter" on your asset. This time, it is your ETF holding instead of your house. The way this works is:

- You sell a call option on the same underlying symbol as your desired ETF.
- The income you bring in by selling the call option lowers your cost basis on the ETF. This also has the effect of lowering your break-even point should the ETF subsequently sell off.
- You already own the ETF, so you don't need to do anything with it.

Note that if you do not currently own the ETF, you can buy it at the same time, in the same transaction. It results in the same position. Some brokers call this a "buy-write" instead of a covered call because you are doing both transactions simultaneously.

Let's look at it like we did the ETF trade, but this time, we will sell a call option with 40 days until expiration at the $55 strike price, bringing in $1.50 per option.

When we say that we bring in $1.50 per option, remember that there is an options multiplier (typically 100, as in 100 shares of the ETF) that we have to multiply the option value by. So if we sell the option for $1.50, we bring in $150.00 per option.

Since we own 1,000 shares of the ETF in this example, we can sell ten contracts in this "covered" example—the ETF "covers" the short call's potential risk to your brokerage firm.

Table A.2: Selling a Short Call

ETF Price	ETF P/L	Short Call P/L	Combined Net P/L (@expiration)
$60	$10,000	($3,500)	$6,500
$55	$5,000	$1,500	$6,500
$50	breakeven	$1,500	$1,500
$48.50	($1,500)	$1,500	$0
$45	($5,000)	$1,500	($3,500)
$40	($10,000)	$1,500	($8,500)
$0	($50,000)	$1,500	($48,500)

As you can see in Table A.2, the income that you bring in from selling the short call caps your maximum possible gain, but provides some downside protection as the ETF drops. How much downside protection? The amount that the call is sold for, $1.50 per option. With the ETF at $50 per share, minus the $1.50 we sold the call for, our new, lower break-even price is $48.50 per share!

Figure A.2 shows the risk and reward graph of the covered call, with the ETF price on the horizontal axis and the profit/loss in dollars on the vertical axis.

Figure A.2

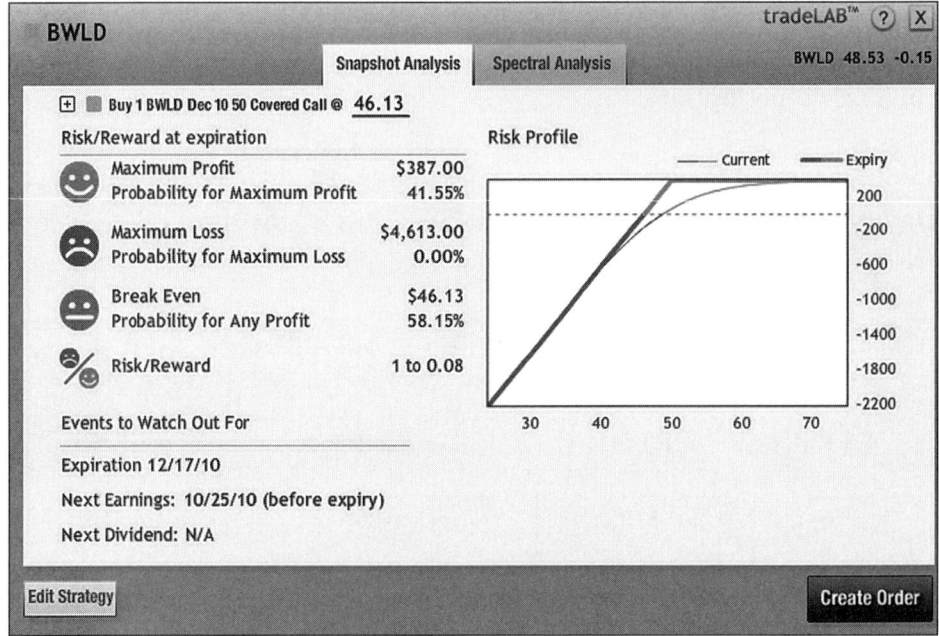

Covered call risk and reward. | Courtesy tradeMONSTER

Risks

In either of these cases, as you can see from the tables, you have to be at least moderately bullish on the prospects of the ETF. If not, the best trade is to exit the position entirely. The income you bring in provides a small amount of downside protection, but does not insulate you from a big downside move.

Rewards

Covered call trades can bring in additional income if an ETF stays in the same place or rallies. But those gains are capped once the ETF starts trading above the strike price you have sold.

In our example above, if the ETF goes nowhere—just stays at $50 a share—you keep the $1,500 for the sold call. Divide that $1,500 into the $50,000 that the ETF holding is worth, and you can see that for about a month and a half (40 days), you have a three percent return. Huge winner? Nope. But a consistent trade that works well in slowly upward-grinding markets (or ETFs); this is a strategy you can put to work month in, month out.

That is an A-to-Z look at the most basic and widely used option trade, but I like to take it a step further. Using your newly obtained knowledge of covered calls, let's talk about my favorite strategy using ETF options—diagonal spreads.

WHAT MAKES A DIAGONAL SPREAD DIFFERENT?

I am sure that all the explanation of the covered call was review for many of you. What does this have to do with diagonal spreads, you ask? It's simple: a diagonal spread is simply a covered call, but you exchange the ETF holding for a longer-term option.

In my case, I use deep in-the-money (ITM) options in place of the ETF itself. I chose this because it costs less, but also moves more like the ETF than an at-the-money (ATM) call option. In options parlance, ITM options have a higher delta than ATM options. This simply means that when the ETF moves up or down by $1.00, these ITM options will move more than the ATM options will.

Table A.3: Diagonal Spread

	Cost	Max Gain	Max Loss
Long 1000 shares at $50	$50,000	infinite	$50,000
Long 10 contracts at $6.50 per option	$6,500	infinite	$6,500

If we look at a simple exchange of the ETF for an option expiring roughly six months from the time of this writing, and find a delta higher than 70 percent, it leads us to the $42 strike price, expiring in March 2011. This option is quoted at about $6.50 per option. See Table A.3.

Comparing Long ETF with a Deep-In-The-Money Call Option

Let's first compare the ETF against the new long option.

Figure A.3 shows how the long option looks on a risk graph.

Since the options will gain 70¢ of the next $1.00 gain in the ETF (and each $1 thereafter, a little more than 70¢), this seems to be substantially better utilization of your trading capital, with one exception. If this is an ETF you intend (or are required) to hold for a very long time, then owning the ETF is a better alternative.

Figure A.3

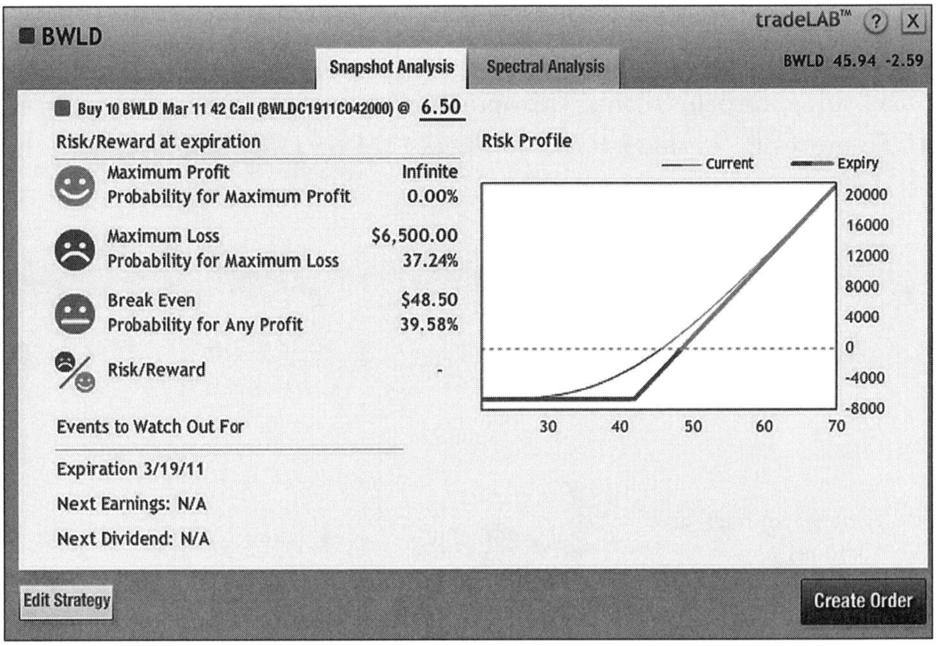

Long option risk graph. | Courtesy tradeMONSTER

Speaking Diagonally

Let's recap what we've covered to this point, and then we will tie it all together.

1. Covered calls give an equity investor the ability to bring in immediate income on their ETF or ETF holdings. In our example above, a roughly three percent yield was demonstrated.
2. A deep in-the-money call behaves very similarly to (but not exactly like) an ETF position.
3. A diagonal spread uses a deep-in-the-money call option as a substitute for an ETF.

So what does this thing look like when we pull it all together? See Table A.4.

- We are still going to sell the December 50 call option for $1.00.
- Instead of buying the ETF for $50 per share, we will buy the March 42 call for $6.50.

Table A.4: Diagonal Spread Trade

Buy Mar 42 call	$6.50
Sell Dec 50 call	($1.00)
Net debit for diagonal spread	$5.50
Options Multiplier (100 shares per contract)	$550 per spread
[times] 10 contracts (ea.) to equal 1,000 shares	**$5,500 total risk**

Figure A.4

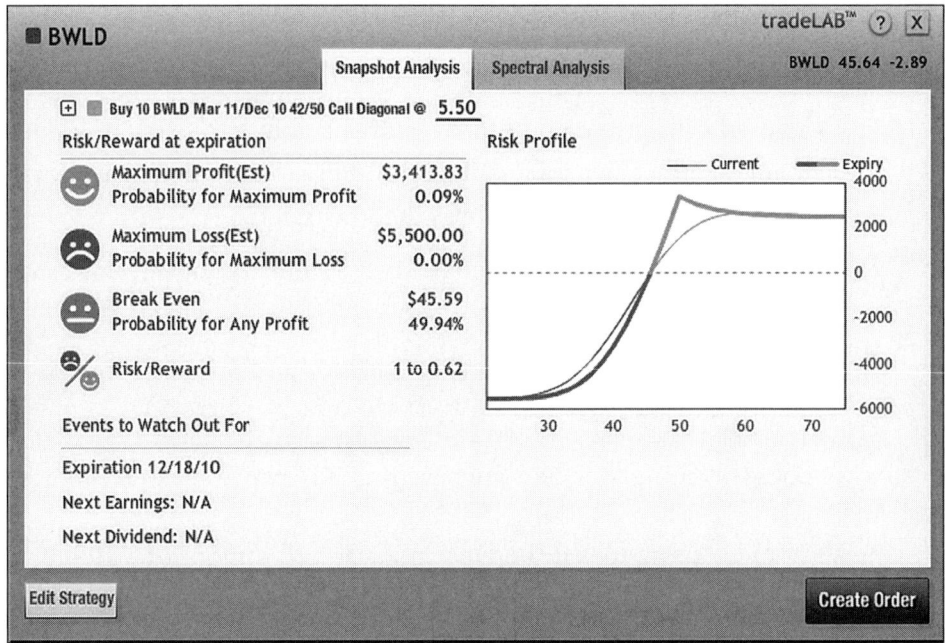

Digonal spread snapshot analysis. | Courtesy tradeMONSTER

Figure A.4 presents the same information in a snapshot analysis.

From the snapshot overview of the position, you can see here that the highest potential profit for this trade happens at December expiration if the ETF happens to be trading at exactly the strike price of the short option ($50). If we were to hold it that long, there is a theoretically possible 62 percent return on this trade instead of the 3 percent that we had with the covered call.

So…62 percent versus 3 percent. Why no exclamation points? Why no huge bold text saying "WOW!"

Because this is extremely unlikely to happen. The way that I view these trades is that if we can get a 20 to 30 percent return, we are going to take the profits, exit the trade, and look for another opportunity. When might that be possible?

Figure A.5

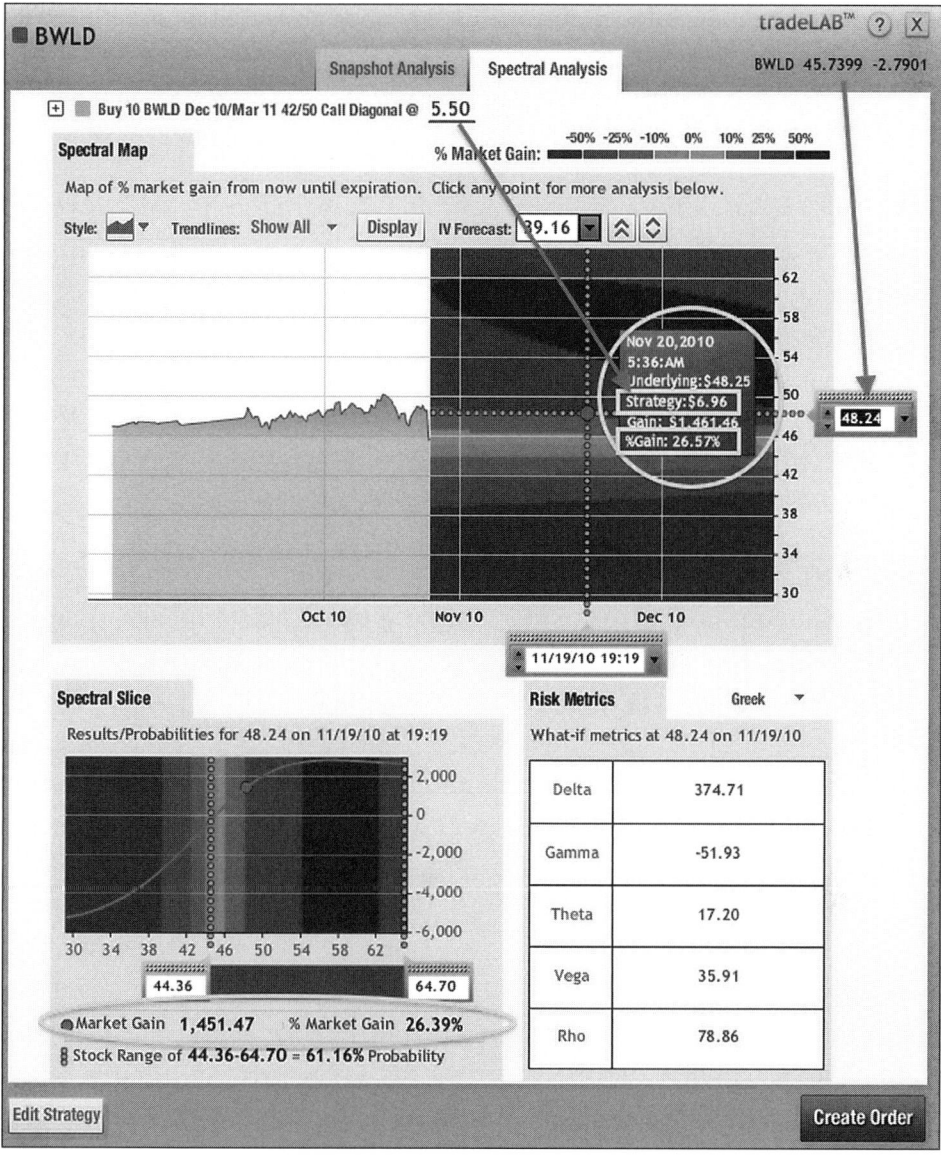

Spectral analysis. | Courtesy tradeMONSTER

Figure A.5 shows the very cool Spectral Analysis tool that online broker tradeMONSTER has available for this trade. Let's take a look and see what it can show us.

Two ETF Options Strategies

In Figure A.5, instead of the simple analysis we have been looking at throughout the paper, we can "what-if" every combination of ETF price, volatility assumption, and date between today and the expiration of the short call. The top image actually plots nearly 30,000 data points and shows us where our potential profit and loss is.

We can see that if this ETF retests its mid-October highs by mid-November and returns to $48.24 per share (from the $45.74 you can see it is currently trading at in the top right corner), we would be looking at roughly a $1,400 profit, or 25 percent gain compared to the $5,500 invested.

Also, note in the bottom left of the image, our break-even point on this trade is approximately $44.50, so we have some downside protection on this trade as well.

Exiting the Trade

One important note is that you should put the diagonal on and take it off as a package, on one order ticket. If you enter the trade with ten contracts, you might take a few of them off and leave the rest a little longer.

But do not buy back the short calls and leave the long call on unless you're rolling that short call to the next month. You should only do this because the chart is telling you it still makes sense, not just because the trade worked out the last time you tried it.

Better utilization of your trading capital, higher probability of winners, and superior returns compared to covered calls. Diagonal spreads have many situations where they can succeed, and it is well worth your time and attention to learn this winning ETF options strategy.

SIMPLE ETF OPTIONS STRATEGY

There are a variety of option trading strategies in addition to the few that we have already discussed. I utilize diagonal spreads as mentioned above, but more frequently use this next very simple strategy. When it comes to the bread and butter of profits, this is it for me. I recommend keeping it simple with a consistent, conservative approach. It is called using options as an ETF (stock) substitute, which I will explain in detail below.

Options are portfolio insurance; they were created to provide cost effective ways to mitigate downside risk. An option is an instrument that gives the owner the right but not the obligation to buy (a call) or sell (a put) option on an underlying ETF, index, or futures contract at a set price for a particular period of time, usually a few months. Remember, an investor buys a call option if he thinks the underlying investment will rise in value. He buys a put option when he thinks the underlying investment will fall.

My DVD set, *ETF Elements* (www.etfelements.com), combines a simple trading system with a simple options system that focuses on buying in-the-money options. Other options are at-the-money (ATM), and out-of-the-money (OTM), but ITMs are generally the optimum selection. They provide leverage for your capital while reducing risk. To explain the "In-The-Money as an ETF Substitute" concept more clearly, let's take a look at Figure A.6.

This example shows the costs and return associated with buying 100 shares of ETF versus buying one contract (which controls 100 shares) of an ITM

Figure A.6

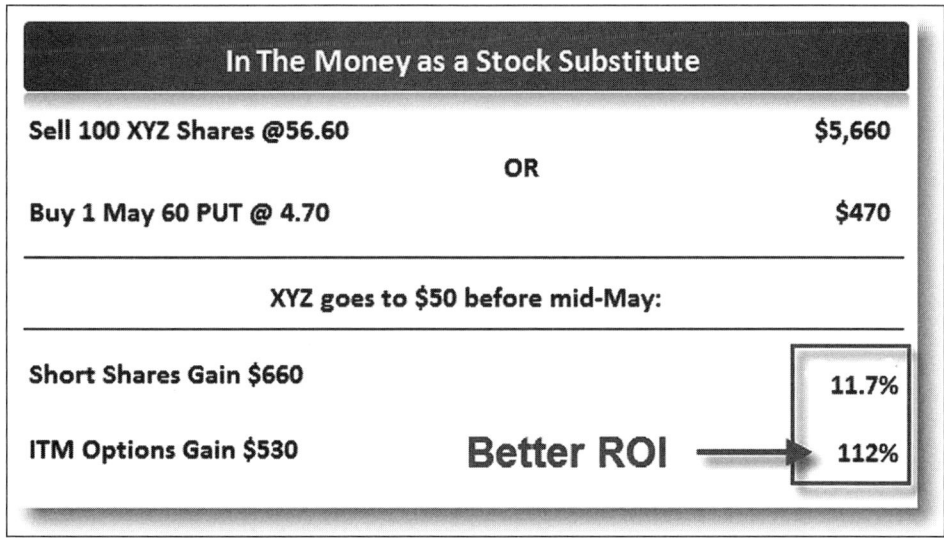

In-the-money substitute.

Two ETF Options Strategies

option. An investor can obtain a much higher return on his investment (ROI) with this simple options strategy—investing only one-tenth as much in the ITM options can provide ten times the return on the investment. Furthermore, by investing less capital on each trade, you can afford to trade multiple ETFs simultaneously, and this can provide much needed diversification and additional opportunity.

CONCLUSION

Regardless of which strategy you prefer—ETF Diagonal Spreads, or ETF Options as an ETF Substitute—you will find better utilization of your trading capital, higher probability of winners, and superior returns compared to trading the ETFs alone.

Trade well,

Andrew Hart
ETF Analyst | BigTrends.com

RECOMMENDED READING

CHAPTER 1

Ferri, Richard A. *The ETF Book: All You Need to Know About Exchange-Traded Funds.* Hoboken: John Wiley & Sons, 2007.

Hill, Joanne and George Foster. *Understanding Returns of Leveraged and Inverse Funds.* Journal of Indexes, September/October 2009.

CHAPTER 2

Carr, Michael. *Smarter Investing in Any Economy: The Definitive Guide to Relative Strength Investing.* Cedar Falls: W&A Publishing, 2008.

Kirkpatrick, Charles. *Beat the Market: Invest by Knowing What Stocks to Buy and What Stocks to Sell.* Upper Saddle River: Pearson Education, FT Press, 2008.

CHAPTER 3

Brooks, John. *Mastering Technical Analysis: Using the Tools of Technical Analysis for Profitable Trading.* New York: McGraw-Hill, 2005.

Edwards, Robert D. and John Magee. *Technical Analysis of Stock Trends*, 7th edition. AMACOM, 1997.

CHAPTER 4

Dorsey, Thomas. *Point & Figure Charting: The Essential Application for Forecasting and Tracking Market Prices.* Hoboken: John Wiley & Sons, 1995.

CHAPTER 5

Daley, Paul, Phil Dorencz, and Dan Bargerstock. *ETF Liquidity Explained*. Journal of Indexes, March/April 2010.

Murphy, John J. *Technical Analysis of the Financial Markets: A Comprehensive Guide to Trading Methods and Applications.* New York: New York Institute of Finance, 1999.

"Chatting with Marc Chaikin." *Technical Analysis of Stocks and Commodities*, v. 12:1 (30-37).

CHAPTER 7

Faith, Curtis. *Way of the Turtle: The Secret Methods that Turned Ordinary People into Legendary Traders.* New York: McGraw-Hill, 2007.

Hardin, Thomas L. *Investor Revolution! Overthrow Wall Street and Take Back Your Future*. Indianapolis: Literary Architects, 2007.

CHAPTER 8

Douglas, Mark. *Trading in the Zone*. New York: Prentice Hall Press, 2001.

Steenbarger, Dr. Brett N. *The Daily Trading Coach: 101 Lessons for Becoming Your Own Trading Psychologist*. Hoboken, New Jersey: John Wiley & Sons, 2009.

▲▲▲▲▲▲

To get the current lowest price on any item listed
Go to www.traderslibrary.com

Glossary

Advance/Decline Line: The most widely used method of evaluating market participation; a market-breadth indicator that compares the advancing stocks on the NYSE to the declining stocks.

Asset Allocation: Percent of cash, bonds, and stock in a portfolio.

Backtest: To use historical data in order to determine past performance of a particular trading methodology.

Commodity Futures Trading Commission (CFTC): The independent federal agency established by the U.S. Congress under a major revision of the Commodity Exchange Act. The CFTC has an overall responsibility to regulate the futures industry in the United States.

Divergence: The comparison of the security's price to technical indicators. A divergence occurs when the indicator is moving in the opposite direction from the price of the security.

ETF: Exchange-traded fund. A security that combines elements of index funds with a twist by pooling securities that track specific market indexes at a very low cost. ETFs represent ownership in an underlying portfolio of securities that tracks a specific market index.

ETN: Exchange-traded note. Like ETFs, but backed by the credit of the issuing bank rather than by portfolio holdings.

Fidelity Sector Fund: Mutual funds launched by Fidelity investments during the 1980s which allowed traders to profit from sector rotation. These funds catered to traders by offering hourly pricing.

Flash Crash: When the market briefly plunged 1,000 points on May 6, 2010.

Leveraged ETF: Fund designed to achieve a multiple of index returns on a daily basis. For example, a double-leveraged long fund will move twice as fast as the index it tracks. A double-leveraged short fund will move twice as fast and in the opposite direction from the index it tracks.

MACD: Moving Average Convergence/Divergence Indicator. Developed by Gerald Appel, MACD is a price momentum indicator that plots two lines. The price phase line represents the difference between two moving averages and is the fast line on the indicator. The signal line is a moving average of the price phase line.

Market Timing: Essentially, being in when the market rises and exiting when it falls.

Modern Portfolio Theory: First introduced by Harry Markowitz, this theory states that one can generate a higher return with less portfolio fluctuation when the investments in one's portfolio work together.

Money Flow: A running total of an accumulation factor which measures whether the security is being accumulated or distributed by big-money players. See formula on page 90.

Morningstar™ Box: A nine-square grid that classifies securities by size along the vertical axis and by value and growth characteristics along the horizontal axis. Introduced in 1992 to help investors determine the investment style of a fund.

Portfolio Thermostat™: A tool developed by Canterbury Investment Management to help maintain a trader's level of comfort with market volatility. As investments get more volatile (i.e., heat up), tactics are used to cool the portfolio down to where it is comfortable. As volatility declines (i.e., cools off), adjustments are made to heat the portfolio back up.

Rectangle Pattern: A pattern formed on a chart when a security fluctuates back and forth in a narrow range. One horizontal line is drawn connecting the highs, representing resistance, and another horizontal line is drawn connecting the lows, representing support.

Reduced Risk Portfolio: Invests in high-yielding income-based securities. This portfolio holds better-rated vehicles that offer yields well above the money market and CD rates. See www.etfportfolios.net for more information.

Relative Strength: An indicator used by technical analysts to gauge the momentum of a particular stock by measuring its price change over time and comparing it to the change in a major market index, typically the S&P 500. A stock's relative strength is expressed as a percentage that represents how it performs against other securities. For example, if a stock has a relative strength of 60, it has outperformed 60 percent of the other stocks over a certain period, usually 12 months. Some analysts consider high relative strength a bullish indicator of future price increases, while others view it as a sign that the stock is "overbought" and ripe for a correction. Also called price persistence.

Relative Strength Index (RSI): A technical indicator that attempts to determine the dominance of buyers or sellers in the marketplace by using the following equation:

$$RSI = 100 - 100 / 1 + RS \text{ (Relative Strength)}$$

The two thresholds, 70 and 30, mark the boundaries of what is considered "normal" market behavior and what is considered "extreme" in which one side of the market is in complete, if not overwhelming, control. These extreme levels are referred to as "overbought" (when buyers have maximum control) and "oversold" (when sellers have maximum control) conditions.

Resistance: A price level where selling often takes place.

Right Triangle Pattern: A chart pattern that exhibits a series of narrower price fluctuations. On one side of the fluctuation, the boundary of price action is horizontal. The boundary on the other side slopes toward the opposite (horizontal) boundary.

RSMD: Relative Strength using the MACD indicator; measures the momentum of relative strength. See Formula on page 108.

Sector ETF: An ETF related to a certain sector of the market, such as banking, semiconductors, or health care. Less diversified and offering a higher profit potential than the style indexes, sector ETFs began trading in the early 2000s.

Spread: The difference between the bid and ask prices.

Style Index Portfolio: Rotates to the best-performing market segments. This program is for long-term growth by holding broad-based equity ETFs. See www.etfportfolios.net for more information.

Support: A price level where buying often takes place.

Symmetrical Triangle Pattern: A chart pattern that has two sloping trend lines in opposite directions that form two sides of the triangle and intersect somewhere around the middle of the existing price range.

Tactical Allocation Portfolio: Designed to be an "all-weather" portfolio, one that can do well in any market environment. See www.etfportfolios.net for more information.

Triple-Top Buy: A bullish pattern in which two rally attempts fail at the same level, but on the next attempt, the security rises above the resistance level.

Triple-Bottom Sell: A bearish pattern in which the security falls, but finds support at the same area, and on the next attempt, it falls below the previous lows, registering its sell signal.

VApct: Volume Accumulation Percent or Money Flow Oscillator. Developed by analyst Marc Chaikin, this indicator combines volume readings with the relationship between the closing price and the day's price range to reward securities that close near their daily high on above-average volume.

Volatility Managed Portfolio: Innovative approach to limit levels of volatility within a portfolio while maintaining diversification and allowing for growth.

Wedge Pattern: A chart pattern that has two sloping trend lines in an upward or downward direction towards an intersection as the range of daily prices narrows.

About David Vomund

David Vomund is the president of Vomund Investment Management, LLC, a fee-only investment management firm. David has over twenty years of investment experience. Originally a stock manager, he turned to exchange-traded funds (ETFs) long before their mainstream popularity and began exclusively using ETFs for client portfolios in 2003. He also publishes the weekly VISAlert.com newsletter.

David is a frequent speaker at national investment conferences, and his analysis and forecasts have appeared in many publications, such as *USA Today* and *Investor's Business Daily*. He was the featured interview in the October 1999 issue of *Technical Analysis of Stocks & Commodities* magazine.

David holds a degree in economics from the University of California, Davis and an MBA in finance from California State University, East Bay.

You can follow David's postings at www.twitter.com/etfportfolios, on Facebook at Vomund Investment Management, or online at ETFportfolios.net.

THE NEW TL BLOG

Invest in your trading education with the Traders' Library Blog!

New articles and postings added DAILY by some of the greatest minds in trading:

- Sylvain Vervoort
- Steve Palmquist
- Chuck Hughes
- Michael Jardine
- Deron Wagner
- And many more…

A one stop shop for all that is trading; chapter excerpts, eBook downloads, educational videos, updates on upcoming events and products, plus some fun stuff too!

CHECK IT OUT NOW!
blog.traderslibrary.com
START INVESTING IN YOUR FUTURE!

Marketplace Books is the preeminent publisher of trading, investing, and finance educational material. We produce professional books, DVDs, courses, and electronic books (ebooks) that showcase the exceptional talent working in the investment world today. Started in 1993, Marketplace Books grew out of the realization that mainstream publishers were not meeting the demand of the trading and investment community. Capitalizing on the access we had through our distribution partner Traders' Library, Marketplace Books was launched, and today publishes the top authors in the industry—household names like Jack Schwager, Oliver Velez, Larry McMillan, Sheldon Natenberg, Jim Bittman, Martin Pring, and Jeff Cooper are just the beginning. We are actively acquiring some of the brightest new minds in the industry including technician Jeff Greenblatt and programmers Jean Folger and Lee Leibfarth.

From the beginning student to the professional trader, our goal is to continually provide the highest quality resources for those who want an active role in the world of finance. Our products focus on strategic information and cutting edge research to give our readers the best education possible. We are at the forefront of digital publishing and are actively pursuing innovative ways to deliver content. At our Traders' Forum events, our readers get the chance to learn and mingle with our top authors in a way unprecedented in the industry. Our titles have been translated in most major world languages and can be shipped all over the globe thanks to our preferred online bookstore, TradersLibrary.com.

Visit us today at:

www.marketplacebooks.com & www.traderslibrary.com

This book, and other great products, are available at significantly discounted prices. They make great gifts for your customers, clients, and staff. For more information on these long-lasting, cost-effective premiums, please call (800) 272-2855, or email us at sales@traderslibrary.com.